Colonial Homes
in
North Carolina

Colonial Homes in North Carolina

By
John V. Allcott

*Professor of Art
University of North Carolina*

A Publication of
The Carolina Charter Tercentenary Commission
Raleigh, North Carolina
1963
Reprinted by
Division of Archives and History
North Carolina Department of Cultural Resources
1975

DEPARTMENT OF CULTURAL RESOURCES
Grace J. Rohrer, *Secretary*

DIVISION OF ARCHIVES AND HISTORY
Larry E. Tise, *Acting Director*

NORTH CAROLINA HISTORICAL COMMISSION
T. Harry Gatton, *Chairman*

Gertrude S. Carraway J. C. Knowles
Helen G. Edmonds Robert M. Lineberger
Frontis W. Johnston Edward W. Phifer, Jr.

The Carolina Charter Tercentenary Commission was established by the North Carolina General Assembly to "make plans and develop a program for celebration of the tercentenary of the granting of the Carolina Charter of 1663. . . ." As part of this program the commission arranged for the publication of a number of historical pamphlets for use in stimulating interest in the study of North Carolina history during the period 1663-1763. This publication was part of that project.

CONTENTS

	Page
Foreword	vii
Introduction	viii
Acknowledgments	ix

CHAPTER

I. Colonial North Carolina Seen from the Air— *Old Maps of the State and of Colonial Towns* 1

II. A Visit to a Colonial Home 18

III. Kinds of Construction—*Log Houses, Houses with a Wooden Frame, Brick and Stone Houses, Roofs* 26

IV. Plan Ideas—*The Study of Floor Plans* 55

V. Interiors 84

VI. A Note on Later Colonial Architecture 96

VII. The Study of Old Architecture 101

FOREWORD

The following statement was published in the original printing of *Colonial Homes of North Carolina*: "The Carolina Charter Tercentenary Commission was established by the North Carolina General Assembly 'to make plans and develop a program for celebration of the tercentenary of the granting of the Carolina Charter of 1663. . . .' As part of this program the Commission arranged for the publication of a number of historical pamphlets for use in stimulating interest in the study of North Carolina history during the period 1663-1763. This publication is part of that project." Because of the widespread acceptance of this particular pamphlet and continuing demand for it, the Division of Archives and History of the North Carolina Department of Cultural Resources is reprinting it. When the Carolina Charter Tercentenary Commission went out of existence at the end of 1663, its stock of publications was turned over to what was then the State Department of Archives and History. Since that time several of the pamphlets originally published by the commission have been reprinted.

Because of monetary limitations, it has not been possible to update this publication. Readers should be aware of the fact that a number of projects in progress at the time Dr. Allcott wrote the booklet, such as the Museum of Early Southern Decorative Arts in Winston-Salem and Tryon Palace in New Bern, have been completed.

Chairman of the Carolina Charter Tercentenary Commission was the Honorable Francis E. Winslow of Rocky Mount; executive secretary was Brig. Gen. John D. F. Phillips, U.S. Army (Ret.).

The awareness of the importance of structures of historical significance has increased with the recent emphasis on historic preservation. It is appropriate, therefore, that Dr. John V. Allcott's work on North Carolina's colonial homes be kept in print.

         Memory F. Mitchell
         Historical Publications Administrator

July 1, 1975

INTRODUCTION

This booklet, planned for young student readers, discusses a group of colonial homes scattered over North Carolina, which remain and can be seen today. They begin in the early 18th century, for earlier homes have long since disappeared. The fate of these first buildings is likewise the fate of most of the churches, courthouses, and other non-domestic structures built during colonial times. Homes, therefore, chiefly constitute the first group or body of architecture remaining from the early and mid-18th century.

Architecture of the final years of the colonial period will be mentioned only lightly. During this later time new ideas of elegance came into North Carolina architecture, as in the well known Tryon Palace, to which we will refer later. For many people who have not thought very much about colonial architecture, these elegant later buildings, and also those of the early Republic, stand somehow for all or the best of "colonial" architecture, and the exciting architecture of an earlier, bustling, genuinely colonial period is not recognized. It will be useful in this booklet, therefore, to focus on the architecture of the earlier 18th century and see the simple, vigorous ideas of this period.

These buildings are of surprising variety—they are made of brick, stone, or wood; they are large and small, plain or fancy in one way or another. A reason for such diversity is that the colonists, coming from different foreign countries and settlements in America, brought with them differing ideas about what a building should look like and how it should be constructed. These early buildings, however, do hold together as a group. More important, they show the rise of architectural ideas especially suited to the hot Carolina summers. Thus, we view our material both as expressive of a genuine "colonial" period, and as establishing ideas which reflect Southern life.

Besides talking about colonial architecture as an important aspect of colonial history, this booklet has two special purposes. One is to interest the student in architecture itself. Some people go through their whole lives without ever being conscious about buildings they like or dislike; they do not wonder why one building looks gay, another sober, and others pompous or unpretentious. This study will provide a number of approaches to architecture. Using everyday vision, so to speak, we will see photographs of buildings from outside and inside, in long-shot and close-up. We will see buildings in plan views and diagrams which show in a few lines what a photograph cannot. We will look down on buildings and cities from high in the air (via maps). And we will look with X-ray eyes into the construction of buildings. In these and other ways a person begins to experience the manifold realities of architecture and to understand how architecture ranks with painting and sculpture as a great, compelling art. Buildings and cities are the material frame created by man, in which he can breathe and live life as he desires it.

The other special purpose of this booklet is to induce the student to investigate old buildings in his or her area—to find them, prowl through their basements and attics to see how they were made, make sketches and take photos of them, look up records, and talk to old citizens about them. People who do this are detectives in a sense; it may take months before the mysteries of a particular building are solved. This is very important work. Each day old buildings are destroyed without any record for architectural history. Such a record can be made only by someone on the spot over an extended period of time—someone like the reader of this study.

ACKNOWLEDGMENTS

In this booklet we enter the world of two dedicated students of North Carolina architecture, Professor Louise Hall of Duke University, and Mr. W. S. Tarlton, Superintendent of the Historic Sites Division of the State Department of Archives and History. The manuscript was read by Professor Hall and Mr. Tarlton, and also by Professor Joseph C. Sloane and Miss Priscilla Roetzel, two of the author's colleagues at the University of North Carolina, and by General John D. F. Phillips, Executive Secretary of the Carolina Charter Tercentenary Commission. These people, warmly interested in our project, made numerous important suggestions which are reflected in the present booklet. Other North Carolinians have aided our study of individual buildings:— Mr. Donald Carrow and Don Carrow Jr., of Bath; Mrs. Guy Springle, Miss Annie L. Morton, Mr. and Mrs. Henry Hatsell, and Mr. and Mrs. Marlin Reed of Beaufort; Dr. and Mrs. William Wassink of Camden; Dr. William Jacocks, Mrs. Jane Bahnsen, and Mr. William Powell of Chapel Hill; Miss Mary Louise Phillips of Charlotte; Miss Elizabeth Vann Moore and Mr. David Warren of Edenton; Mr. and Mrs. John M. Stuart of Elizabeth City; Mr. and Mrs. L. A. Chenoweth, near Hertford; Mr. and Mrs. Chester Haworth of High Point; Dr. Mary Claire Engstrom and Mrs. Edward Lloyd of Hillsboro; Miss Gertrude S. Carraway, Mr. and Mrs. Tull Richardson, and Mr. William F. Ward of New Bern; Mr. George W. Alexander of Nixonton; Mrs. Sprague Silver and Miss Sue Todd of Raleigh; Mr. Frank L. Horton of Salem; Mrs. Henry Fairley, Sr., and Mr. William D. Kizziah of Salisbury; Mrs. Katherine N. McCall of Southern Pines; Mr. Edmund H. Harding of Washington; the Misses Eleanora and Joanna MacMillan, near Wilmington; Mrs.

Peter Rascoe of Windsor; and Mr. Henry Jay MacMillan of Wilmington.

Illustrations in this booklet are gratefully acknowledged below. Figures 21, 24, 31, 33 and 60 are photographs by Frances Benjamin Johnston. These photographs, and also photographs 67 and 70, the maps, figures 1, 2, and 49, and photostats of maps, figures 3, 4, and 10, are in the Carolina Room, The University of North Carolina Library. Other photographs come from State agencies in Raleigh: figures 12, 13, and 48 are from the Department of Conservation and Development, and figures 11, 28, 57, 58, 59 and 62 from the Department of Archives and History. Of other photographs, figure 27 is from Old Salem, Inc.; figures 15, 32, and 36 are by William Brinkhous; figure 35, from Mrs. John M. Stuart; figure 71 is by William H. Jennings and is used with his permission. Figure 5 is used with permission of Harcourt, Brace and Company. Figure 25 is reproduced by permission of Harvard University Press. Other photographs and drawings are by the author.

CHAPTER I

Colonial North Carolina Seen from the Air

We begin our study from the air. First, like an astronaut high in his rocket ship, we will look down on colonial maps of North Carolina and survey the whole 500-mile sweep of the land from mountains in the west to meandering sea coast in the east. Next, as if in an airplane, we will look at maps of colonial towns. Then, coming closer to the earth, as in a helicopter, we will hover over a single home with its several outbuildings and see what it is like. From this point on, with our feet on the ground, we will look at buildings close-up.

OLD MAPS OF NORTH CAROLINA

There are quite a number of old maps of North Carolina. Some are small—the size of a piece of typing paper; others are huge—assemblages of several large sheets of paper. Early maps, not very accurate in detail, show a few settlements. Later maps are more accurate and show the new towns as they were established.

Back of a colonial map stands a surveyor who travelled over the land making careful drawings. He made the map for the King or other official of government, for mariners or merchants, or for people like ourselves who are curious about life on the land. These maps suggest the life of the colonists, and their architecture, as will be seen.

The study of North Carolina maps has been facilitated by a recent book, *The Southeast in Early Maps*, by William P. Cumming. Mr. Cumming, a professor at Davidson College, spent many years searching for maps in the libraries of our country and Europe. Much of the information and inspiration for this booklet comes from his work.

One point before we begin looking at maps—words are often "misspelled." This happens because some words (as Indian names) were new and spelling had to be invented for them. There are other reasons, the most appealing one being that eighteenth-century writers enjoyed a freedom about spelling.

Figure 1, "A New & Accurate Map of North . . . Carolina . . ." is a detail from a map of southeastern North America, "drawn from late Surveys . . . by Eman. Bowen." This map was included in a geography book which Bowen published in London in 1747. The scale of our illustration is slightly smaller than that of the original map.

The map gives a grand and sober image of the New World. In the west are the great "Charokee Mountains." Individual peaks are shaded on one side, making them seem massive and solid as they thrust up forcibly from the land. At the eastern side of the range are little trees, delicate signs of green timber growth. Big letters tell us that "Virginia" is at the north, "North Carolina" is in the middle area, and "South" indicates the beginning of South Carolina, below. A meandering, dotted line bounds North Carolina, which was not considered as extensive then, as it is today.

In the middle and upper part of the map many rivers

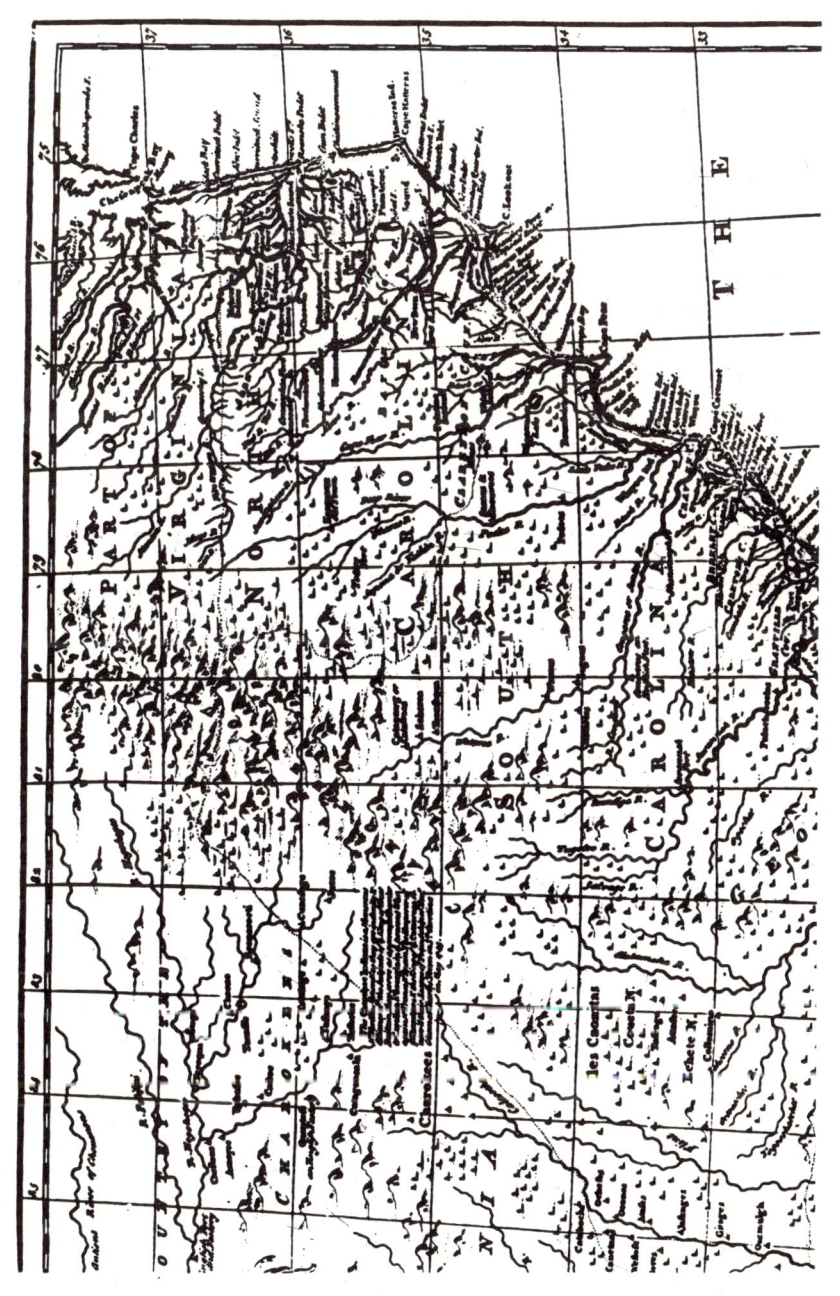

FIGURE 1. DETAIL FROM "A NEW & ACCURATE MAP OF NORTH . . . CAROLINA," LONDON, 1747.

begin their courses to the sea. Six or seven of them may be counted. They fan out as they flow onward, the upper ones moving to the east, the lower ones more to the south. Fatter and wider they become, finally creating Albemarle Sound, "Pamticoe" Sound, and other features of the intricate shore line. The sounds and wide river mouths provided good places for small ships to land and for towns to be established. Light vessels could push far up some of the rivers, and farmers and planters along the banks could ship from their own private docks.

This seaboard area is densely labeled with names of places, an indication of the extensive settlement of the region. Follow down the coast, and one finds Edenton, Bath Town, New Bern, Beaufort Town, and farther to the south are Wilmington and Brunswick Town. All these places were founded well within the first half of the 18th century. Those who spend vacations at Topsail Beach, Hatteras, Ocracoke, and other Carolina beaches, will be surprised at the number of such places which had already been given their names by 1747. To the west of our map are unfamiliar Indian names of forts and settlements. Others have English-sounding names. This map of 1747 does not show towns like Hillsboro and Halifax, founded in the 1750's, nor towns farther west, like Salem, Salisbury, and Charlotte, founded in the 1760's. In studying early maps like this, one can feel the westward growth of North Carolina in colonial times.

Since the map is rather small, it does not show all of the settlements which did exist at its time, 1747. For example, Campbell Town, which later became part of Fayetteville, is not shown. Our mapmaker, Mr. Bowen, was too high in the air, so to speak, to note this place and hundreds of individual farms. To see in greater detail the richness of life on the land below, we will descend lower in our next map.

FIGURE 2. ALBEMARLE SOUND REGION, FROM "MAP OF NORTH AND SOUTH CAROLINA . . . ." MOUZON, 1775.

Figure 2, the Albemarle Sound region, is a detail from a famous map of North and South Carolina by Henry Mouzon, Jr., made in 1775. Like the previous map, it was printed in England and is also reproduced in slightly smaller size than the original. Mr. Cumming states that it may be called the Revolutionary War map of North and South Carolina, because it was used by American, British and French forces. So, in looking at the fragment, reproduced here, a person might imagine that he is a Revolutionary War general, studying the little towns, the ports, and roads that wander through the country, and try to understand why a town is where it is, what military importance it has, or how it might be protected or destroyed.

Through Albemarle Sound runs a dotted line indicating the course for ships. It may be seen where they could escape to or enter from the Atlantic through the narrow, hazardous Roanoke Inlet.

At the left, near where the Chowan River empties into the Sound, is the town of Edenton. Several roads came together here, and the little black rectangles suggest buildings. There is a church in the town, with a tower and steeple in front. Other churches shown elsewhere on the map have exactly the same form as the one at Edenton, so one realizes that this form is not meant to show what a specific church looked like, but is a standard symbol for a church. Incidentally, notice how churches or chapels stand alone at various places in the countryside.

Courthouses, like churches, are shown in towns, and here and there in the country. They are indicted by a symbol which could be described as a letter "U" which is squared rather than rounded. The courthouse at Edenton is hard to identify; one can not be sure about it.

To the northeast of Edenton, on the Perquimans River, is

the town of *Hartford,* now called Hertford. Farther to the east is Nixonton, its houses lying along both sides of a single road. Follow the road to the south and see the farms which lie along Little River. Each farm is marked by a spot representing the house, and carries the name of the owner—the names Morris, Evans, Ancoup, and so on, can be read. In the north, above this area, is the Great Dismal Swamp, looking very great and dismal indeed.

Vivid as this map proves to be, we have not seen individual towns very clearly. To get sharper ideas about them, we descend lower to the earth and look at maps of individual towns.

MAPS OF COLONIAL TOWNS—TOWN PLANS

A map of a town shows streets and broad avenues crossing and interlacing in some pattern, wide or narrow lots in rows along streets, and buildings which are placed at the front or deep within the lots. Such matters make one section of a town look different from another and are part of the design or the *plan* of a town.

Lewis Mumford, a man who has a great interest in cities and towns and who has written a number of books on them, considers a town as a work of art. He believes that just as a picture is a work of art, and a house is a work of art, so is a town. The design of a town—the arrangement of streets and lots—expresses the ideas of the people about the right framework in which a good life can be lived.

For our study of colonial towns we are fortunate in having beautiful maps of ten North Carolina towns, all made by the surveyor Claude Joseph Sauthier. The Hillsboro map, figure 3, is one of these drawings. Sauthier traveled over North Carolina between 1768 and 1770, surveyed and made maps of Bath, Beaufort, Brunswick, Edenton, Cross Creek (now

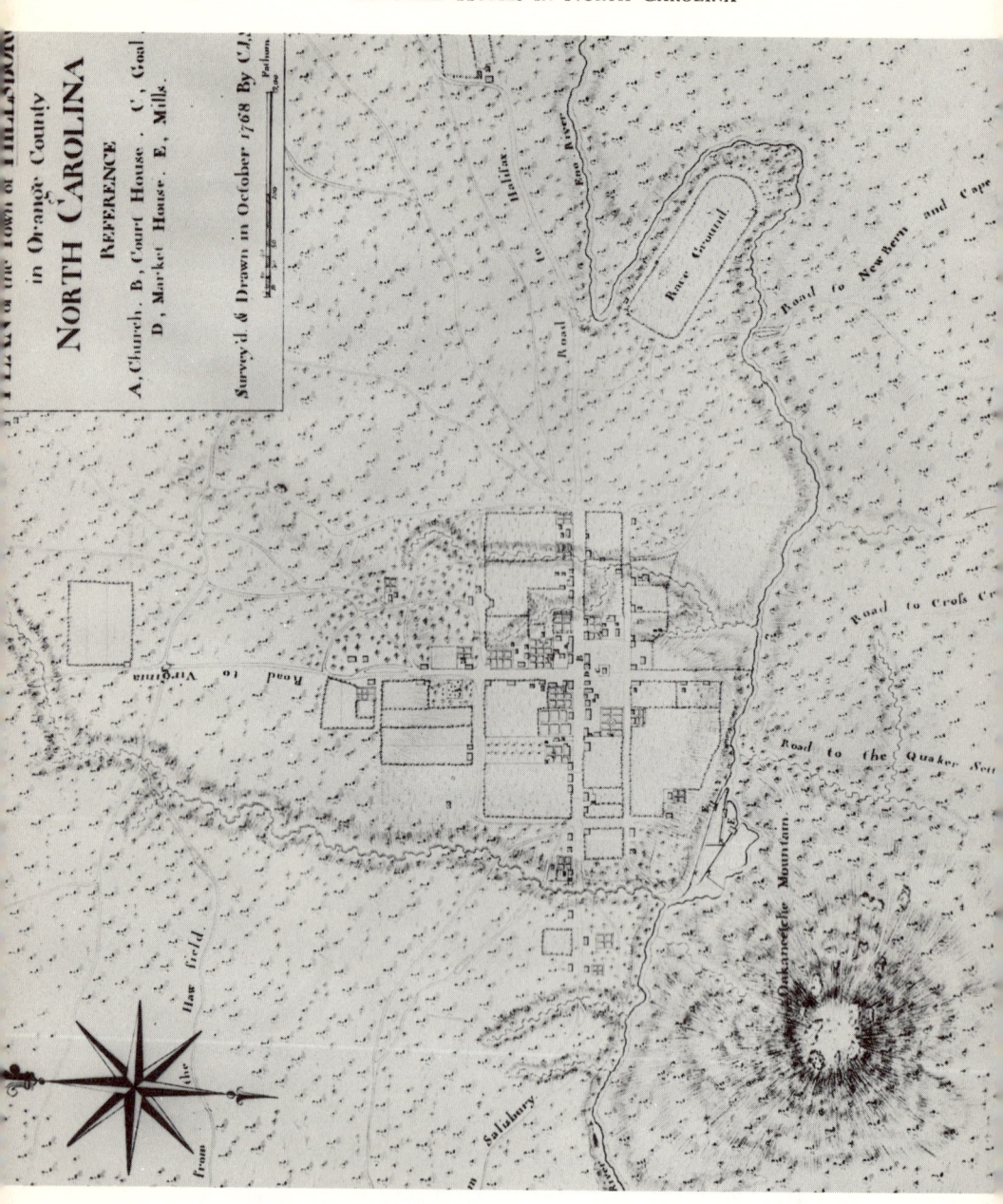

FIGURE 3. SAUTHER'S "PLAN OF . . . . HILLSBOROUGH," 1768.

Fayetteville, Halifax, Hillsboro, New Bern, Salisbury, and Wilmington. The drawings were commissioned by Governor Tryon; most of them have found their way to the great British Museum, in London.

The majority of the buildings shown on the maps have disappeared. The maps thus enable us to see—what otherwise we could never see—North Carolina towns as they once were. Sauthier did make occasional mistakes; and some details (for example, the design of a flower garden) are not to be read as literal fact; but for the most part the drawings may be studied as aerial photographs. By great good fortune they were made at the right time for us, and have survived.

To get some general ideas about colonial towns, we will look at the map of Hillsboro. Our remarks about this map reflect observations of Dr. Mary Claire Engstrom, scholar of 18th-century subjects, and a vice-president of the Hillsboro Historical Society. The Sauthier map of Hillsboro, dated October 1768, was made after the spring uprising of the Regulators in that town and immediately following Governor Tryon's arrival there in September. From this it may be suspected that, in commissioning the map, Governor Tryon had military thoughts in mind. Hillsboro—the danger spot— was the first map in Sauthier's series of ten maps. The others were made as he travelled with Governor Tryon.

The little town is shown on the Eno River in the wooded land of Orange County. The big star at upper left shows north, south, east, and west, and one notes that the town seems to be laid out "properly" on these directions. Roads leading to neighboring towns are carefully marked. There are the Roads from Salisbury . . . to Virginia . . . to Halifax . . . to New Bern . . . to the Quaker Settlement . . . to Cross Creek. At lower left is "Oakaneetche Mountain," a great hump of earth overlooking Hillsboro. Another of the Occoneechee mountains is seen at the edge of the map. The Occoneechee Indians were one of several Indian tribes in the area. Today, boy scouts in this part of Orange County belong to the Occoneechee Council. They sometimes have camporees at the Hillsboro race ground, not far from the "Race Ground" marked on our map. This Race Ground lies neatly within a bend in the Eno River, as though the river wanted to mark out this area of flat land for such special use. Scattered here and there outside the town are farms. The rectangular plots of farm land are clearly marked, and the farm houses and secondary buildings are placed at corners convenient to the road.

For a better view of the actual town itself we look at an enlarged section of the map, Figure 4. Buildings are indicated by small rectangles which have heavy outlines on two sides—the right side and the lower side. These two heavy lines may be regarded as a shadow cast by the bulk of the building. They are a convention used by Sauthier to show bulk or mass. The various rectangles which are shown within gardens also employ this same thick-thin line convention, suggesting a mass of green foliage rising above the surrounding paths.

The buildings marked "A," . . . "B," . . . "C," and so on, are identified under corresponding letters listed under "Reference" at the upper right of the total map. "A, Church" is toward the northern part of the town, removed from the business area below. In assigning to the Church the "A" (number one) position on his list, Sauthier pays respect to the idea of the primacy of the spiritual order over civil law. At "A" is a rectangle containing a number of crosses. This seems to suggest a fenced-off cemetery. One does not find an actual church building, but a church did exist on this ground shortly after Sauthier's visit.

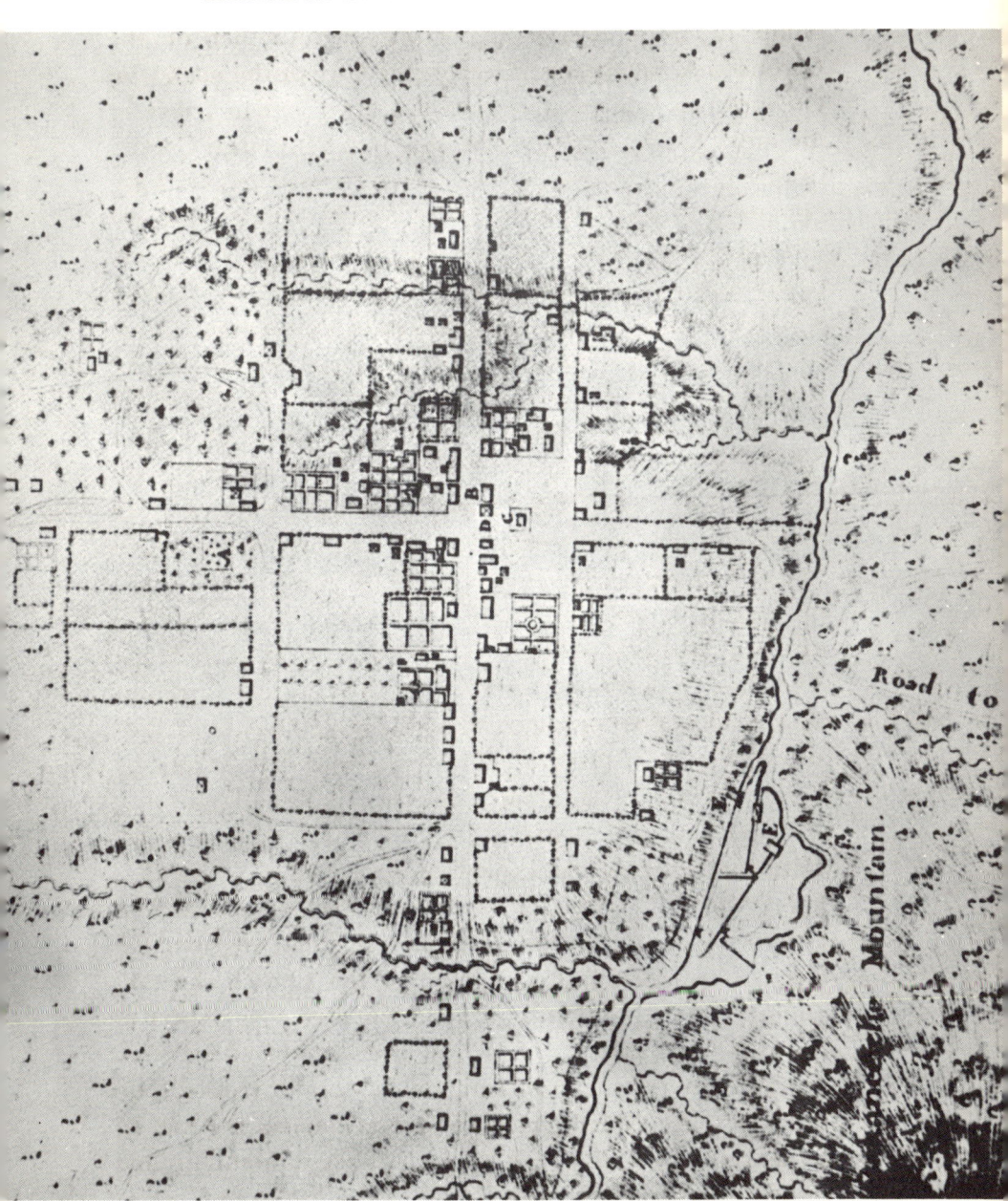

FIGURE 4. DETAIL FROM SAUTHIER'S PLAN OF HILLSBOROUGH.

"B, Court House" is located close to the crossing of two wide streets—those two main streets from which roads lead off to the other towns of the Colony. The courthouse was a "plain, barn-like structure." The present and very famous Old Courthouse, dating from near the mid-19th century, stands near this site.

"C" marks the jail. The word *jail* used to be spelled *gaol,* but Sauthier spells it *goal*. It is shown within a small rectangle, perhaps indicating a fenced-in yard. The jail may possibly have been a new structure, for Dr. Engstrom has discovered that about six months before Sauthier's visit a former jail, at another location down town, was sold to a private individual to use for business purposes. The new jail was probably not an impressive building, perhaps only a log cabin, but Sauthier thought it important to note that the town had this institution to take care of wayward people. Incidentally, the jail seems a little wayward itself, having strayed into the otherwise clear, wide street. When the jail was built that street was perhaps just a well worn path, and the jail may have been erected hastily without careful checking of stakes for the street. In other colonial towns (for example, in the placement of the church at Bath) it sometimes seems as though buildings are incorrectly placed. The Hillsboro jail, for many years in the general position shown, has recently been moved back to a less assertive site.

"D, Market House," directly at the main intersection and adjacent to the courthouse, is shown as square. The "X" inscribed within this square perhaps indicates that the market had a pyramidal, four-sided roof. The building may have had open sides, like markets in certain other colonial towns. The open market building is an idea brought from Europe. Other buildings around this main intersection were stores or warehouses. At the southwest corner was Johnston and

Thackston's store where Edmund Fanning, the Clerk of Court and a Tory leader, took refuge from the Regulators in 1770.

At "E, Mills" there are curious parallel straight lines which can be read as canals. The mills, probably with water wheels, are built over the canals. Where the river widens out at the left there may have been a dam to hold back the flow of water in the river, and force it through the canals. The curious marks on the canals could be gates.

The mills are the last structures identified on the map. Sauthier does not mention the Commons, a field set aside for pasturing of the cattle owned by people in a colonial town. On some of his other maps he identifies such places as Tann Yard, . . . School House, . . . Tobacco Store, . . . Windmill.

The homes shown in the map are all built near the street. Behind are fields or gardens divided into orderly plots. Most of the buildings are simple rectangles in shape. Occasionally a building has an irregular shape, perhaps meaning that an original rectangular structure was given an addition. Similarly, lots with irregular shape may indicate additions or subdivision of an original tract.

By way of contrast to the Hillsboro town plan, Figure 5 is a drawing of Grenoble, a medieval French city. This drawing is reproduced from *The Culture of Cities,* by Lewis Mumford. The winding streets are natural paths that have become fixed as streets. Some curving streets mark the location of early town walls, removed as the town grew and as larger encircling walls were erected. Mr. Mumford speaks of this kind of town as having a natural circular plan, with irregular blocks dictated by topography and the original circular wall.

When American colonial towns like Hillsboro were founded, the streets and lots were laid out in advance. The

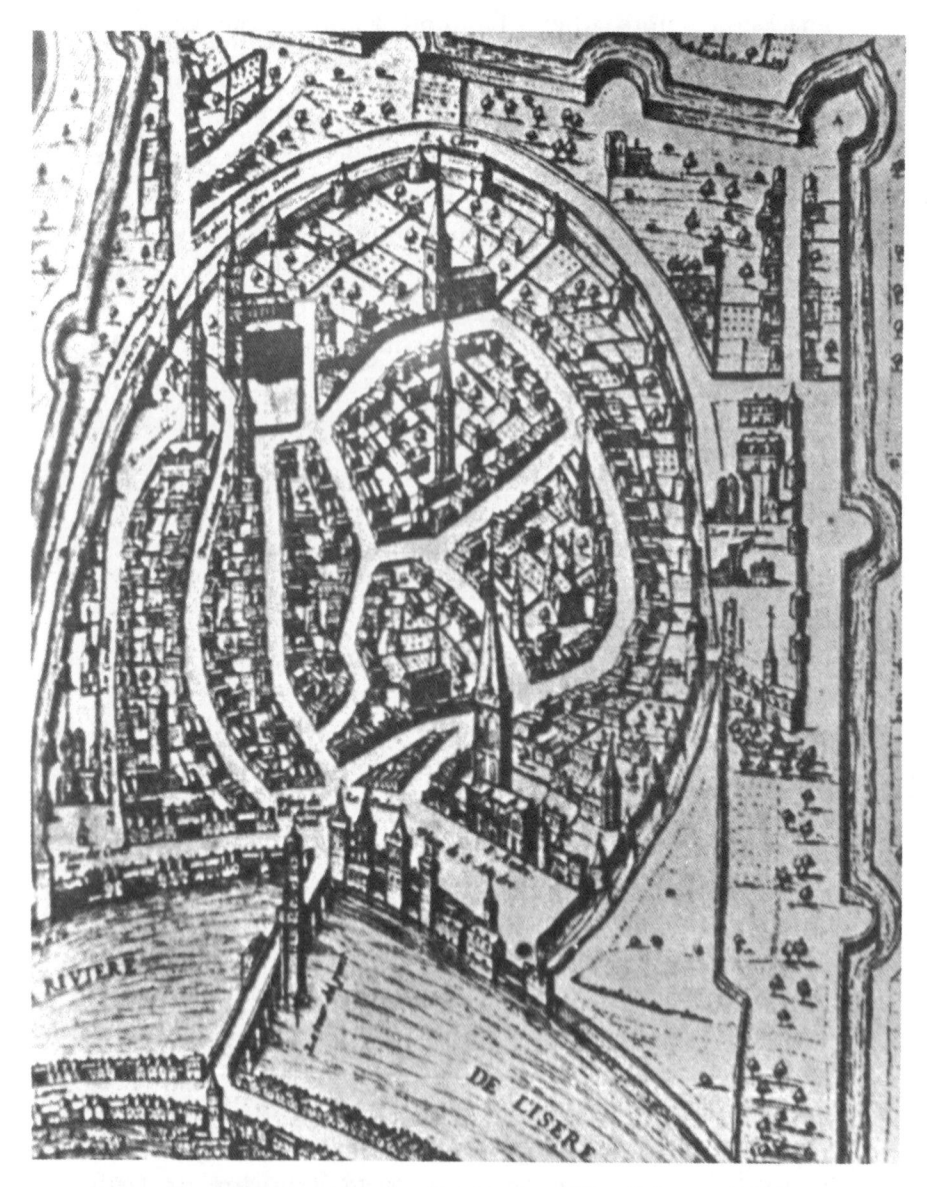

FIGURE 5. MAP OF GRENOBLE, FRANCE, FROM *The Culture of Cities* BY LEWIS MUMFORD.

uniform rectangular lots were easy to measure and ideal for fixing sale prices and for the assessment of taxes. Later expansion of the town could also be orderly. The idea of the colonial gridiron town speaks of "modern" men and their institutions, as opposed to medieval men.

Figures 6, 7, and 8 suggest planning ideas found in early North Carolina towns. Figure 6, recalling Hillsboro, could be called a plan for an inland town. In our diagram two slightly wider streets mark a crossing at the center of the town. The dot in the center of the crossing is to indicate the placement of the courthouse. Such placement is not what we saw at Hillsboro, but is shown on several of the Sauthier maps of North Carolina towns (for example, Salisbury and Wilmington). This was a good arrangement, for the courthouse, symbol of the civil law and order of the area, might be seen from a long way off as the town was approached from various directions. However, the early towns which began with the courthouse astride the main crossing generally found later that this location impeded the flow of traffic. Consequently, some courthouses have been moved from their original sites, allowing traffic to flow across the intersection. Pittsboro, however—although a relatively late colonial town, having been laid out in 1785—still has its courthouse in the central position.

Figure 7, to suggest the plan of a port town, seems like half of the inland plan, above. A principal street of the town runs along or near the water. It might be called Water Street, as at Bath.

Figure 8 indicates an idea found at Salem, laid out in 1765, and elsewhere in the American colonies. A central square is left open and principal town buildings are built around it. At Raleigh, laid out in 1792, the square is very large, and contains the State Capitol. A central green be-

FIGURE 6.

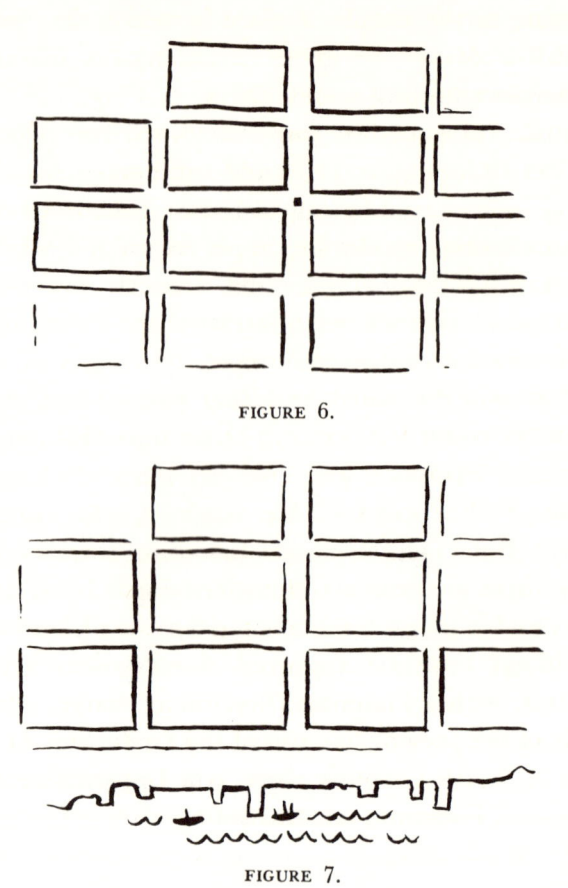

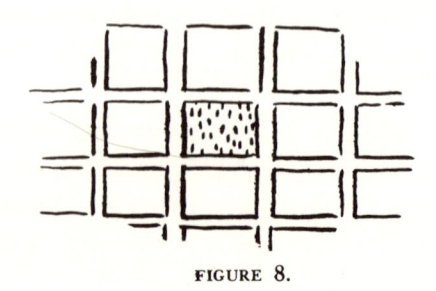

FIGURE 7.

FIGURE 8.

longing to the people, a place in which they might gather, is still a pleasant reminder of community life and order in those towns which possess them.

Since colonial days our old towns have changed much. In the 19th century mills and warehouses dwarfed the original buildings. The railroad, that glamorous invention of the industrial revolution, appeared in the towns, bisecting them. Especially in the 20th century, faster change and "progress" have all but obliterated the charm of old towns. Downtown streets become impossibly congested. Old residential areas are invaded by filling stations and supermarkets. In a free country a man can buy a beautiful old home, blast it out of existence, and erect an unsightly factory over its ruins. Such "progress" has blighted and disfigured many towns. But townspeople are becoming horrified by this, and now there are citizen committees which bring about zoning laws under which the plans for the use of land and for new buildings must be approved. Some towns have Planning Boards, with a Planning Director in charge, who think not only of the present but also of the far future. At the University of North Carolina there is a Department of City and Regional Planning; it trains young men and women for positions in planning.

CHAPTER II

A Visit to a Colonial Home

FIGURE 9. CONJECTURAL SKETCH OF THE PALMER HOUSE, BATH.

After looking at maps of North Carolina and its towns, we visit a colonial home to see what it is like. The Palmer-Marsh house in Bath is chosen for this purpose because it offers exceptional possibilities for the kind of visit we want to make.

Figure 9 is a sketch of the big, sturdy house, its out-buildings, orchard, and gardens which, taken together, look like a self-sufficient farm. Our sketch of the surroundings is an estimate, based on the plan of the "Col. Palmer" property seen in Sauthier's 1769 map of Bath (figure 10). The map shows the Palmer property "down town" on Water, or Main Street, which runs along Bath Creek, the house being placed directly on this business thoroughfare. The front room of the house was planned for business purposes, and so it has its own door to the street. Thus the chimney, which ordinarily would have been on this end wall, has been moved around the corner to the side. The house, thought to have been built in 1744, was sold to Colonel Palmer in 1764, just a few years before Sauthier came to Bath.

Of the four out-buildings in a group, a well house is in the foreground. The drawing shows the well covered by a

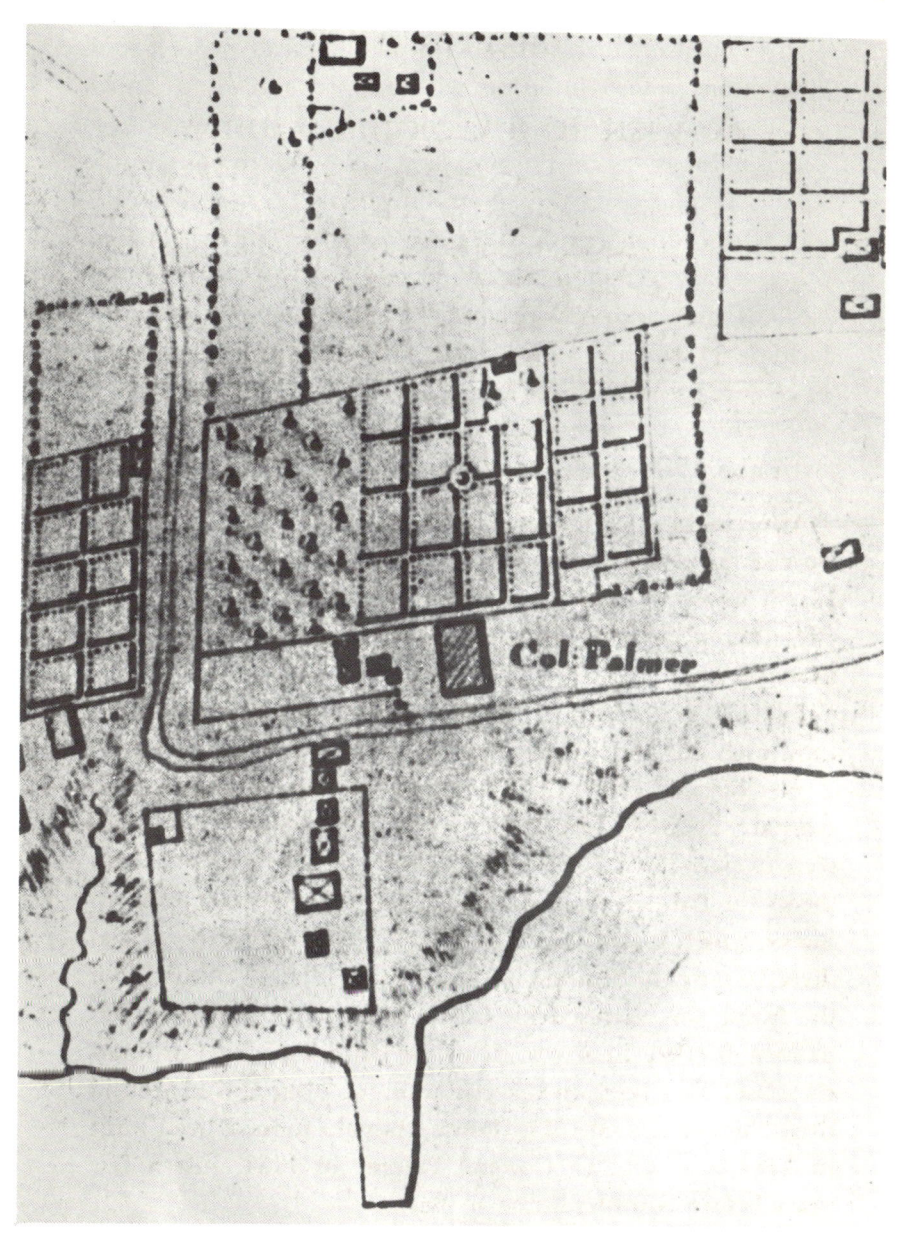

FIGURE 10. (BELOW), COL. PALMER'S HOUSE, SEEN IN A DETAIL FROM SAUTHIER'S "PLAN OF BATH, 1769."

square, open-sided structure with pyramidal or hipped roof. The other square building with hipped roof is a smoke house—where meat was hung and smoked. A smoke house which exists today on the property is thought to contain the wood frame of this original structure. Of the two out-buildings with ordinary gable roofs, one could be a dairy and the other a barn. At the back of the property are the extensive gardens and the orchard—represented in such charming fashion on Sauthier's map. We know that in 1911 the yard of the house was full of pear, apple, and other fruit trees, the descendants, perhaps, of the original trees in the orchard.

In the 19th century porches were added to the house (figure 11); but the porches have recently been removed during a project to restore the house to what it originally was (figure 12). The juxtaposition of these two photographs brings the above ideas forcibly to our attention. It is important to know that almost every colonial house has undergone changes during the years, and to know the meaning of conscientious restoration.

In the 19th century the house was "modernized" in several ways. The porches were a very natural addition, especially for hot Carolina summers. The shutters were removed because they were considered archaic. In the windows the small 18th century panes of glass were replaced by larger panes available in the 19th century. Also, the street façade of the house was made more up-to-date, as can be seen. The gable projects emphatically and has two horizontal strips at the lower corners. The gable suggests (vaguely) a pediment on a Greek or Roman temple. (A *pediment* is the low triangular gable end of a classical temple). Note that the supports of the side porch also are classical; they are clean, elegant Doric columns. The classical ideas mentioned above were popular in the post-colonial period.

FIGURE 11. THE PALMER HOUSE BEFORE RESTORATION.

FIGURE 12. AFTER RESTORATION.

By contrast, the restored house of today is much closer to what is characteristic of the earlier 18th century in North Carolina. The whole street façade of the house registers in the viewer's mind as one simple plane, without strong overhang at the top, and without any suggestion of a classical pediment. It is interesting to note that the design and color of the restored shutters are based on one old red shutter found in the attic of the house.

Figure 13 shows the back of the house, with its famous double chimney, an unusual feature rarely found. The windows in the chimney give light to closets on the first and second floors. In the plan of the first floor, figure 14, it may be seen how a closet is placed between two bedrooms, serving one of them. On the floor above, the closet serves the bedrooms on the other side, thus demonstrating a desire to play fair with bedrooms on both sides of the house.

At the front of the house is the room planned for business. At various times through the years it was used for store, courtroom, and parlor. In the center of the house is a large hall room; it has two outside doors, and an open stairway to the second floor. The dotted line (• • •) indicates a great, central beam used in the construction of the house, having the exceptional length of 51 feet. The dashed line (- - -) indicates the former location of a partition; the back bedrooms were lengthened at the expense of the hall. In the recent restoration of the house the location of the original partition was discovered, and it has been restored.

If one compares the plan of the house in figure 14 with that shown on the Sauthier map, figure 10, it is seen at once that the general proportions are not the same. Sauthier made a mistake; he got the main facts, but was unable to take time to measure every single building he showed.

Figure 15 shows an interior of the Palmer house. Glance

FIGURE 13. PALMER HOUSE, SHOWING FAMOUS CHIMNEY.

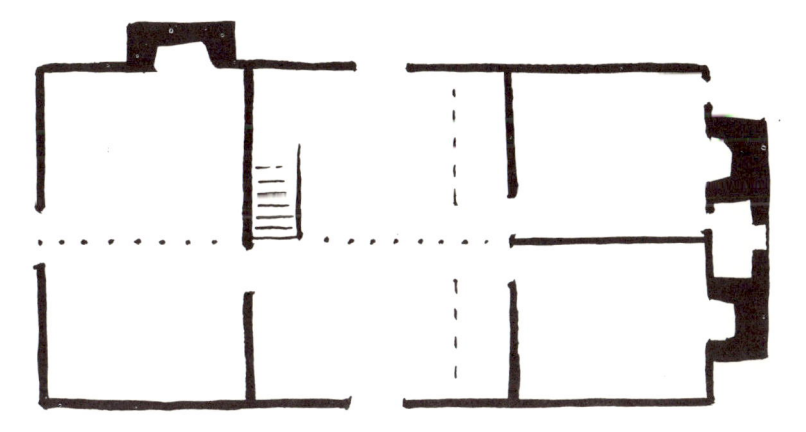

FIGURE 14. PALMER HOUSE, PLAN.

FIGURE 15. PALMER-MARSH HOUSE, INTERIOR.

at the plan, figure 14, and see how this room fits within the total house. Notice the great beam running across the ceiling and, parallel with it, the beam at the side wall. Notice also that the side entrance door is framed at the right by a post which rises to the ceiling. Such exposed beams and posts suggest the wood skeleton of the house. Skeletal structure is concealed in most colonial homes that remain today, but is found occasionally as here in the Palmer house. More will be said later about exposed construction and about interiors.

Our visit to the Palmer house has provided a glimpse into modern, careful restoration. The house was restored by the Historic Bath Commission, in co-operation with The Beaufort County Historical Society, and with assistance from the Historic Sites Division of the North Carolina Department of

Archives and History. The restoration project included much more work than we have shown. For example, archaeological study of old foundations in the yard around the house revealed various uses of the basement and the existence of a 19th-century outside dining rom and kitchen, as was common during this later time.

CHAPTER III

Kinds of Construction

Log Houses, Houses with a Wooden Frame, Brick and Stone Houses

Much of the special charm of a colonial home lies in its structure so quaint and different from the construction used in homes of our day. Some colonial homes are "log cabins," others have a wooden frame or skeleton, and still others are made of brick or stone. Sometimes a builder could choose his materials and kind of construction. At other times and places a builder had little or no choice of materials and was limited to using the simplest tools and construction methods. In order to understand the meaning of colonial architecture one looks carefully at structure.

LOG HOUSES

We begin our study with log houses because they seem the simplest of the several kinds of construction. Log homes or "log cabins" were not built by the first colonists, however. It is true that such houses had been built in northern European countries since very early times, but this type of construction was not introduced in the colonies for houses until late in the 17th century. From that time on, log homes were continuously built in the colonies for pioneer cabins, barns, outdoor kitchens, and other simple structures. In colonial times log construction was also used for jails, forts, and for the first courthouses. We shall note a number of designs for log houses and the various ways in which logs were cut and joined together.

The illustration on page 26 gives the flavor and the feeling of the pioneer log cabin. This drawing of a cabin near Fayetteville is from a travel book, *A Journey in the Slave States, 1856*, written by Frederick Law Olmsted. Olmsted, who won fame as the designer of Central Park, in New York City, was also interested in traveling and seeing how people lived and how they built homes. The drawing shows how the logs fit together at the corners, each log being notched so that it locks with the other logs above and below. The chimney is also made of logs—or, rather, of small sticks—and is plastered inside with mud. The open spaces between the big logs of the house should also be filled or chinked with mud, but Mr. Olmsted observed that they were not. The roof, it will be noticed, is covered with huge shingles, or shakes.

Although there are many log cabins in North Carolina, most of those from the colonial period have disappeared. The Britten Sanders log cabin in Southern Pines (figures 16 and 17), is a well-known example which has survived. It is more elegant than the cabin seen in the preceding sketch. The round logs have been somewhat squared-off. The great chimney is of stone. The roof extends far out on the chimney side to protect clay mortar in the chimney from rain. The clay mortar as well as the clay chinking between the logs has now been replaced with cement for permanence. In the restored chimney it may be observed how the cement does not extend flush to the outside surface. Instead, it is kept

FIGURE 16.

FIGURE 17. LOG CABIN, SOUTHERN PINES.

deep within the stones in imitation of clay mortar which has partially washed away.

The Sanders cabin is a restoration project of the Moore County Historical Association. The Association took the cabin from its original country site and moved it to Southern Pines. The chimney had fallen down, but the stones were picked up and are used in the present chimney. The cabin is on the grounds of the Shaw house, an early 19th-century home. It seems appropriate that the old cabin should be sited on the property of the later house, for this was the practice of the early settlers. After out-growing their first cabin home, they would build a larger house, continuing to utilize the original cabin for cooking, weaving, and other purposes.

In the close-up photograph of the door and wall of the cabin may be seen a latch cord hanging from the door. A row of rafter ends shows just above the door. One rafter end is missing on the right; this marks the point where an inside stair rose to the loft. The present stair and the flooring of the cabin were taken from another old house.

The Blair-McCormack house, near High Point (figures 18, 19 and 20), presents some further ideas about log houses. This building is the Enos Blair log cabin, constructed around 1750, later enlarged, and now the Jimmy McCormack house. The original cabin is surrounded by porches front and back, and additions on the left and right sides. At first glance the house seems quite recent and unremarkable; old log houses do not always reveal themselves in first casual view.

The logs of the cabin are joined as shown in the sketch, figure 19. This joint shows brilliant structural development beyond the simple saddle joint seen in previous examples. The craftsman who chopped the squared log ends had great skill as he cut the intricate geometrical teeth which lock together so securely and accurately. One can imagine him at

FIGURE 18. BLAIR-MCCORMACK, HOUSE NEAR HIGH POINT.

FIGURE 19. DETAIL.

work:—he would cut a joint and lay the log in place. If the joint fit—fine. If it did not quite fit, he would remove the log and make further necessary cuts. This type of joint sheds water very well.

Because of the side additions to the Enos Blair cabin, nowhere around the present house can one see two outside walls as shown in our sketch. However, other cabins in North Carolina do show the complete joint as drawn.

The plan of the original cabin is given in figure 20. It shows what we have not seen before, a chimney completely inside of the house. The chimney, thus protected from rain, is laid with clay mortar. A narrow stairway at one side of the chimney winds up to the loft above. On this stairway the visitor is face to face with the great chimney, and can scoop out a sample of "mortar" with his finger nail, proving that the stones were indeed laid in clay.

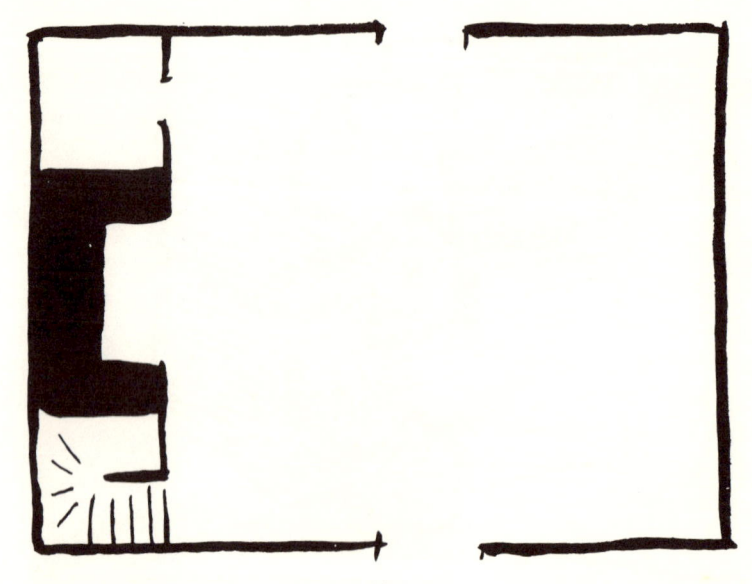

FIGURE 20. PLAN.

Figure 21, the Gregg Cabin, in the mountains of Caldwell County, is a further example of beautiful craftsmanship. The photograph shows changes that time has brought to the original house, but attention should be focussed on the lower walls in the foreground. Here the logs have been cut down to great planks, and so squarely cut that chinking seems almost unnecessary. The design of the corner joint, simpler than that of the Enos Blair cabin, is called "dove-tail"—each plank ends with a shape something like the tail of a dove.

Figures 22 and 23 show designs for double cabins—two cabins under one roof. The first idea, called the *Saddle-Bag* cabin, has two rooms attached to one central chimney. This plan gets its name because it resembles two saddle bags hanging over the back of a horse.

The second design, called the *Dog-Run*, has a chimney on each end, and an open breezeway—or dog run—through

FIGURE 21. THE GREGG CABIN, CALDWELL COUNTY.

FIGURE 22. "SADDLE BAG" CABIN, PLAN.

FIGURE 23. "DOG RUN" CABIN, PLAN.

the center. This plan is also known as the *'Possum Trot*. No doubt the design was a favorite for large families, for it provided an out-door play area for children in good weather and bad.

Look back at the Gregg cabin (figure 21); by study of its roof line the plan of the cabin can be understood and named.

Both the Saddle-Bag and the Dog-Run plans are simple—just two cabins under one long roof. It seems appropriate therefore, that they should be of simple log construction.

Figure 24 is the John Knox cabin in Rowan County, built about 1752 but recently destroyed by fire. This illustration shows interesting developments in design. At first glance the structure does not seem to be a log house at all, but rather a medium sized clapboard house with a porch cut into one corner. But where the clapboards have been torn away one may see chinked log construction underneath. On the surface of this inner wall are vertical strips to which the clapboard siding is nailed. It is not uncommon for log structures to disappear beneath siding added at some later date. With the John Knox cabin we know the siding was added *after* the porch and shed because the siding sweeps without break across the whole side of the structure.

Olmsted noted this kind of cabin on his travels in South Carolina and was very appreciative of its features, which he described in some detail. In cabins of the better type, he said,

> The roof is usually built with a curve, so as to project eight or ten feet beyond the log wall; and a part of this space, exterior to the logs, is inclosed with boards, making an additional small room, —the remainder forms an open porch. The whole cabin is often elevated on four corner posts, two or three feet from the ground, so that air may circulate under it . . . The porch has a railing in front . . . The logs are usually hewn but little, and, of course, as they are laid up, there will be wide interstices between them. They are commonly not 'chinked' or filled up in any way; nor is the wall lined inside.

FIGURE 24. THE JOHN KNOX CABIN.

KINDS OF CONSTRUCTION 37

That such cabins were indeed of a better class becomes painfully clear when Olmsted adds a note about the cabins of poorer people. These cabins were "mere pens of logs, roofed over, provided with a chimney, and usually with a shed of boards, supported by rough posts before the door."

FIGURE 25. 17TH CENTURY FRAMED HOUSES.

WOODEN FRAME HOUSES

Houses with wooden frames or skeletons were built in North Carolina long before the log houses seen above. Framed houses represent a tradition of building dating from medieval times which the colonists brought from Europe.

The earliest framed houses in the South have disappeared almost without a trace, but scholars are able to form general ideas about their nature. For example, figure 25, showing several kinds of framed houses, is from Henry Formans' book, *Architecture in the Old South*. The drawing depicts the kind of wall surfaces which might possibly have been seen in

Jamestown, Virginia, very early in the 17th century. All the houses are of wooden frame construction, either exposed or covered. Houses with framework exposed are called "half-timbered." From left to right in the drawing the houses are described as follows:—half-timber work with brick filling; plaster; weatherboarding or clapboards: half-timber work with plaster; and tile-hung. Several of the houses have a projecting second story. All have steep roofs. Windows are of the hinged casement type, with small pieces of diagonally set glass.

Houses of this general sort—especially those with exposed wooden frame and projecting second story—are frequently shown in illustrations in European history books. In England they are called Jacobean, because of their association with the Jacobean period in 17th-century England which followed the Tudor era.

FIGURE 26. THE BROTHERS HOUSE IN SALEM.

As the 17th century gave way to the 18th, the "medieval" open-framed house was generally supplanted by the house with clapboard siding, like the third house in figure 25. This wall surface offered better protection against rain and cold winds than the open-frame house which leaked on all sides. In the 18th century the use of a projecting second story was discontinued. Larger panes of glass for windows became available in the 18th century, and sliding sash windows, like those noted in the Palmer house, came into general use.

Almost all of the medieval open-frame structures in America have disappeared, but North Carolina still has a remarkable example in the Brothers House in Salem (figure 26). Those who have visited Salem in past years may be surprised to learn this and to see the strange-looking building in our sketch, for they recall no such structure. Instead, the Brothers House is remembered as a simple clapboard building. However, the house was built originally as in our sketch; the clapboards, added in the early 19th century, are currently being removed and the house restored to its original character.

Salem and the Brothers House date from near the end of the colonial period—a time long after colonial builders had generally abandoned the earlier, medieval construction. However, we show the Brothers House because it calls up for us the earlier colonial period with houses now destroyed and forgotten, built in such construction.

The town of Old Salem is a show place in North Carolina, one of those few towns anywhere in our country where a whole early settlement is preserved. Salem was established in 1766 by members of a religious group, the Moravians, who planned their town and their life quite differently from other settlers. For example, the Brothers House, built in 1769, was a place for unmarried men to live and to work at carpentry,

FIGURE 27. THE BROTHERS HOUSE IN SALEM. WORKMAN REMOVING 1826 CLAPBOARDS FROM THE 1769 HALF-TIMBERED WALL.

FIGURE 28. THE PALMER HOUSE, BATH, DURING RESTORATION.

pottery and other trades, and to teach these trades. The house is one of several early structures in Salem built in the medieval way with open timber construction or with wood framework covered by plaster. The builders were aware that wood siding would have given better protection, but it was "the most expensive method of surfacing a house" according to a Salem report of 1768. Therefore, some of the early houses were built in the older way. The curious apron roof encircling the walls above the first story somewhat protected the lower walls from rain and also provided a sheltered path for pedestrians.

In 1786 the house was given a brick addition on the left, and around 1800 was plastered over. Perhaps at this time the apron roof was removed. The plastering was apparently not successful, for in 1826 the weatherboard siding was added and remained until its recent removal.

The photograph, figure 27, was taken in the summer of 1962; it shows a workman removing the siding of 1826. The skeleton of the house is made of great squarish timbers. Toward the right of the photograph may be seen the wooden pegs which hold the timbers together. Bricks are cut as necessary to fit within the wooden framework. The photograph suggests a question which visitors ask:—what holds the brick panels in place and prevents them from falling out? The explanation is simple and shows the cleverness of the designers. The brick panels fit into frames that have been slightly hollowed out on their inner sides. Through the window one has a glimpse of an inside wall. It has exposed timber construction too.

In discussing Old Salem we should note plans for opening a new museum, the Museum of Southern Decorative Arts. The museum will contain a series of rooms secured from 18th-and 19th-century homes. This is a new kind of museum for the South and is another reason for visiting Salem.

Elsewhere than Old Salem all the surviving wooden-frame colonial homes in North Carolina have wooden siding. They were probably planned from the start to have this "modern" siding, and hence their skeleton construction was not quite like that in the Brothers House. In order to get an idea of what the new construction was like, we look at Figure 28. This is the structure previously examined, the Palmer house, during reconstruction. The photograph was taken after the later porch was removed, thus exposing the original wooden frame of the house.

At first glance one might take this to be a 20th century house, with vertical studs and horizontal laths to which plaster has been applied from the inside. Drips of wet plaster show clearly in the photograph. However, a closer look shows that the variously sized and irregularly placed wood members come from an age before factory-cut 2 x 4's. Nevertheless, the preponderance of vertical studs does suggest that the builder had a clear idea of "stud construction" in mind. The studs provide a good nailing surface for the laths inside and the clapboards outside. To speculate on this design is to be dazzled by its beauty and simplicity. The builder must have felt that he was really living in a modern age.

Looking further at the photograph one may visualize the craftsman at work, cutting and fitting his wood together in ingenious ways. At the left is a great vertical post which rises through two stories. It is notched on right and left to hold the horizontal beam which passes behind it. These two members are locked together by wooden pegs. The doors is framed by two thick posts, with two light studs between. The window above the door is also framed by thick posts. But because the window is narrower than the door, it requires only one

Kinds of Construction

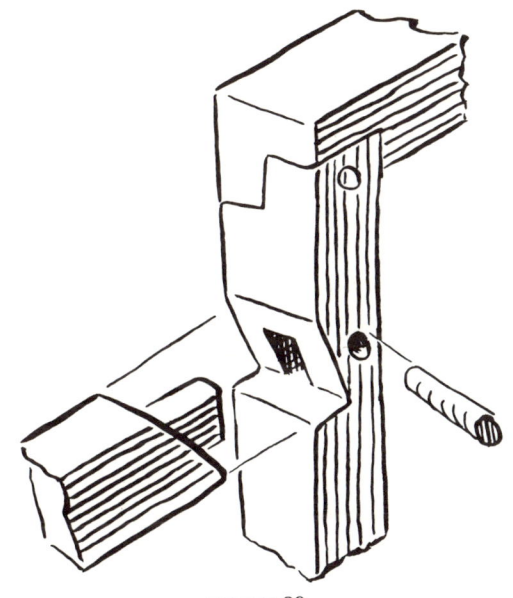

FIGURE 29.

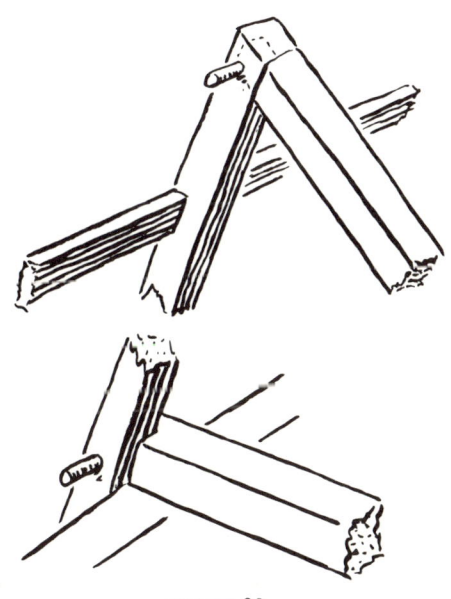

FIGURE 30.

stud between its posts. At the right, a large post is braced by diagonal sticks, one on either side. This post corresponds to the post noted on far left, but that post was made of one long piece of wood, and this one is made of two pieces. Details such as these suggest that the builder "played it by ear"—decided upon joints and bracing as he went along.

Figure 29 is inserted here to suggest the variety of clever ways in which colonial craftsmen fitted wood pieces together. Such junctions are called mortise and tenon joints. They are cut with a chisel and mallet. One can well imagine the satisfaction derived by the craftsman in deciding upon the particular kind of joint to cut. When the two pieces fitted together perfectly, a hole was drilled through them with an auger, a peg was cut and driven into the hole, and the proud workman moved on to the next joint. Sometimes, in details such as windows and cabinets, the pegs are as narrow in diameter as the lead in a pencil, but are fitted so perfectly that one must look hard to find them.

Figure 30 concerns the attic of a colonial house. This diagram shows the fascinating mortised and pegged joints on display at the Sloop Point house, which will be mentioned later. At floor level a rafter is cut and locked with a floor beam. At the ridge of the roof two rafters are beautifully mortised and pegged together.

When visiting an old house, it is often rewarding to ask the owner what he knows about its construction details. Sometimes under a stairway or along a damaged plaster wall one may see into the skeletal structure. Walls are not always hollow as in the Palmer house; sometimes they are filled with brick or clay bats, thus recalling medieval construction. Basements, as well as attics, are good places in which to find hewn joints. On the outside of a house the trim at the corners and at the roof should be studied. The problem on the outside

FIGURE 31. THE CUPOLA HOUSE, EDENTON

is *water*—rain water which may get into the ends of a piece of wood, or into joints, thus causing rotting. This problem should be kept in mind when examining the trim on a house; colonial builders were very aware of it.

Figure 31, the Cupola House in Edenton, is one of the oldest remaining wooden frame houses in North Carolina. It is famous for its exterior with cupola and overhanging second story, and for its interior rooms, lavishly carved. Sauthier's map of Edenton clearly shows the house facing its own wharf on the bay, a fine view of which can still be had from the cupola. The house is dated between 1724, when Richard Sanderson purchased the lot "unimproved," and 1726, when he sold the lot with a house on it. Toward mid-century another owner installed the carved interiors. At present the building serves as the Edenton Public Library.

The overhanging second story supported on brackets recalls the sketches of 17th-century houses previously seen, and the Cupola House has been praised as the finest framed Jacobean house in the South. Our photograph, taken some years ago, shows scalloped shingles around the cupola and ordinary shingles on the roof. The latter are replacements, for, of course, houses have to be reshingled at intervals. Since this photograph was taken the Cupola House has been reshingled completely with scalloped shingles in an effort to restore the original appearance of the roof.

BRICK AND STONE HOUSES

A few early 18th-century brick houses remain in North Carolina. They exhibit a special kind of shimmering beauty. Figure 32, the Jordan farm house, near Windsor, thought to have been built in 1713, is one of the earliest of these houses. It burned in the 1920's, and its new dormers and wood details are not of colonial design, but the original brick mass of the house has been preserved to be seen and enjoyed. The brick surface has a sparkle, a checkerboarding of light and dark, which results from using bricks which are glazed on their ends, but left unglazed on their sides. The bricks are laid in courses in which ends (headers) alternate with sides (stretchers). This system of laying brick is called Flemish bond; it differs from the method used today in which only the stretchers are exposed. The colonists presumably felt that Flemish bond was strong and proper, and they certainly were charmed by the appearance of the walls.

There is a further special effect to be noted in brick houses such as the Jordan house. The chimneys are set inside the wall, and so do not break the smooth outside surface of the wall. The basement, although projecting slightly, is made of the same stuff as the upper wall. Thus the whole lower part of the house registers in one's mind as a very clean,

FIGURE 32. THE JORDAN FARM HOUSE, NEAR WINDSOR.

FIGURE 33. NEWBOLD-WHITE HOUSE, NEAR HERTFORD.

rectilinear form placed directly on the ground. By contrast, framed houses are more complicated in their geometry, with brick chimneys projecting at the sides, and with brick foundations showing in obvious contrast to clapboard walls.

Figure 33, the Newbold-White house near Hertford, is also of the early 18th century, but is smaller and closer to the ground than the Jordan farm. The wooden lean-to on the right is a later addition. This side with three dormer windows was once the front of the house. The base has been plastered over, to protect the brick which at this level often disintegrates.

This picture was made by the master photographer, Frances Benjamin Johnston. It brings out the dazzling brick surface of the old structure and other details of brickwork design, such as the window tops set in gentle arches and the horizontal line which runs across the end wall. This line is a shadow cast by two slightly projecting courses of brick and marks the division between first and second floors; on the inside, the offset courses provide a ledge on which to lay floor beams.

Brick, as may be inferred from above, was used in a number of structural and decorative ways; some are suggested in figure 34. Flemish bond (figure 34a) we have already noted. English bond (34b) has courses entirely of stretchers alternating with courses entirely of headers. This bonding system is illustrated in chimneys from the Palmer house, figure 13, and from the Sloop Point house to be seen later. Sometimes all the bricks in a course were set diagonally, thus producing a remarkable accent line (34c); or the square ends of a row of bricks were molded or rubbed into curves (34d). In some brick houses remaining from the later 18th century, as in the Salisbury area, bold and gay patterns were

Kinds of Construction 49

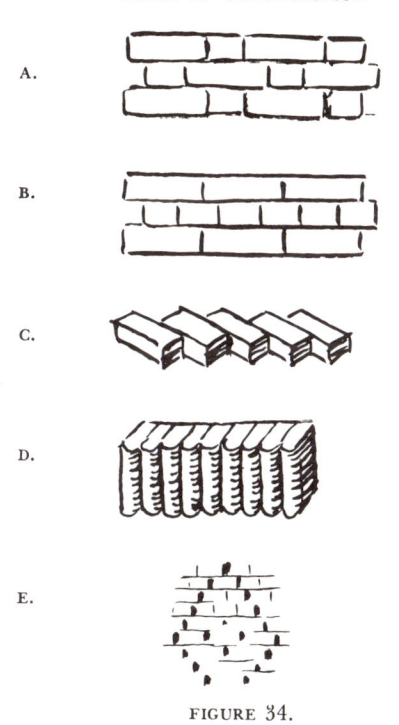

A.
B.
C.
D.
E.

FIGURE 34.

FIGURE 35. THE OLD BRICK HOUSE, ELIZABETH CITY.

created through use of glazed, and lighter and darker bricks (34e).

It may be supposed that masons enjoyed such improvisation, just as woodworkers took pleasure in the design of joints. When visiting a brick house and studying its details, the mortar should be examined also. Sometimes it will be found to contain bits of shells, for the colonists made an inferior sort of lime by burning oyster and other shells.

Figure 35, the Old Brick House, near Elizabeth' City, demonstrates that some colonial houses had chimney walls of brick with front and back walls of wood. This well-known, early 18th-century house stands on the Pasquotank River, which can be seen in the illustration just beyond the house on the right. Not a little of the fame of this beautiful house comes from the legend that Blackbeard the pirate once lived here, mooring his ships at his own landing, nearby.

Each face of the house is clearly symmetrical, bespeaking the sense of balance which was so important to the 18th century. The end walls are in Flemish bond; the walls of the basement are of stone, the indivdual stones being like huge pebbles, rounded by centuries of washing on some beach. Such stones in colonial homes are often called "ballast stones" because sometimes they were shipped over as ballast in vessels from England and other shores. However, there is some doubt that this was so in the case of the present house, because it is unlikely that a ship in ballast could have sailed into the shallow Pasquotank River.

The floor plan and the famous interiors of this house will be discussed later in this booklet.

To be noted along with brick houses are a few stone houses in the Piedmont, remaining from late colonial and early republican times. Figure 36, the Michael Braun house, near Salisbury, built between 1758 and 1766, is an impressive

FIGURE 36. MICHAEL BROWN HOUSE, NEAR SALISBURY.

example. Its orange-hued walls are two feet thick. Some years ago the house was in poor condition, remove this phrase, but was repaired by the Brown (Braun) family. It has now been purchased by the Rowan Museum, Salisbury, and is being restored by that organization.

Like so many of our early houses, the Braun house is unusual in several ways. Immediately striking is the non-symmetrical division of the stone façade, not at all like the Old Brick House and other 18th-century houses. The wooden structure at the right is the kitchen. In the kitchen is a great fireplace along the stone wall of the house, with the chimney containing ingenious flues to heat adjacent rooms in the house. The kitchen is a restoration.

ROOF IDEAS—GABLE, GAMBREL, AND HIPPED

In discussing the structure of colonial homes we add a note on the several kinds of roofs which were used. After a builder had raised the masonry or wood walls of his house, the roof was a major design and construction problem. The type of roof selected represented what the builder thought was good-looking and appropriate for his special needs.

Our diagram, figure 37, shows a *gable* roof on the left, contrasted with a *gambrel* roof on the right, each type having a dormer window to light the attic space thus making it more pleasant and usable. The gable room is simpler in construction, and was the type most generally used in the colonies; but our diagram suggests how it cramps free movement within the attic. The gambrel roof, although calling for more involved construction, affords more head room. Apart from the space consideration, the gambrel roof is rather cheerful and attractive when seen from the outside, a factor that may have been responsible for the 18th-century fad for them.

FIGURE 37.

FIGURE 38.

Both the houses shown in the diagram are called "story-and-a-half." Neither has a full second story like the Palmer house. Many believe that in colonial times the tax on story-and-a-half houses was less than that on two-story houses, and that for this reason people built the former type.

Figure 38 shows the *hipped* roof, in which four roof planes, one on each side of the house, all slope back toward the center above, thus shedding water from all sides. The vertical walls of the house end in a top horizontal line which extends uninterruptedly around the house. Thus the lower part of the house, especially from the standpoint of the little figure on the ground in the illustration, asserts itself as a clean cube. In late colonial and early republican times this effect was much appreciated by enthusiasts of "modern art," but home builders in the earlier 18th century did not show enthusiasm for the hipped roof, perhaps because it reduced the area of living space on the top floor. However, in early 18th-century public buildings, where an attic space was not of great value, the impressive-looking hipped roof was used. This type roof was used also on smoke houses and well houses, as was seen in the Palmer house.

CHAPTER IV

Plan Ideas

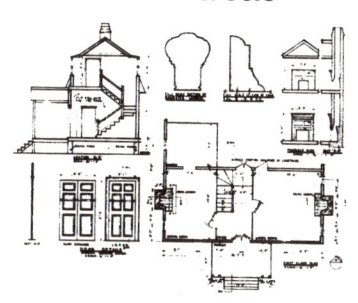

The Study of Floor Plans

The construction schemes we have discussed up to this point—for walls and roofs—have to do with the obvious appearance of a house as it is seen from the outside. But the floor plan of a structure is not such an immediate and recognizable element. It is necessary to go inside a house and wander about in it before one can begin to understand its plan. The plan, however, was clearly in the mind of the builder as he worked; for us, a clear image of the floor plan is important for a full understanding of a building.

The reading of plans is a vivid, very real, architectural experience. For example, let us look at figure 39, a simple one-room cabin. The cabin is entered through one of the doors—doors are indicated by a break in the contour line. The heroic character of the great fireplace is sensed—the fireplace and masonry walls are shown by heavy lines. Opposite the fireplace is found a window—windows are shown by a thin segment of contour line. As one walk up the stairs, turning at the corner, the lines fade away as the level of another floor is approached.

The above experience began with lines on paper and ended by "seeing" the house in three-dimensional space. This

FIGURE 39.

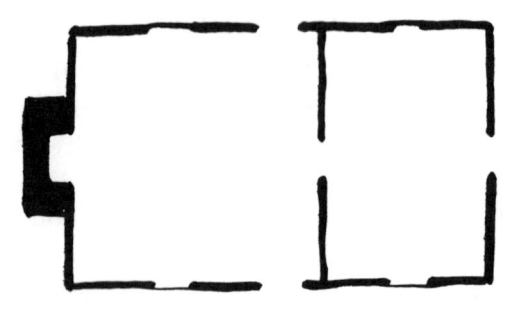

FIGURE 40.

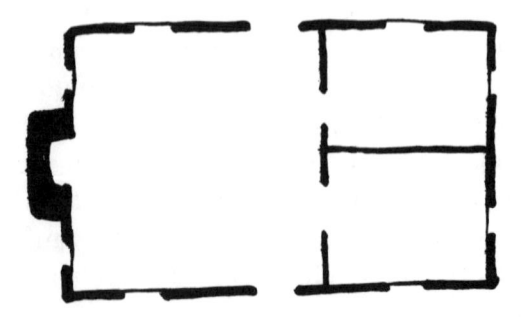

FIGURE 41.

happens in reverse when a house is actually visited. As the rooms through which one moves become more familiar, gradually the floor plan takes shape. This plan can be retained in the mind and can easily be drawn on paper. When the plan is known, much thinking and talking about a building can be done.

SIMPLE FLOOR PLANS

Figures 39 to 45 show a number of first floor plans found in North Carolina colonial homes. Figure 39, which we have already "visited," begins the series with the simplest one-room plan. It is something like the Blair cabin, already seen (figure 20), except for the chimney built inside the house in the earlier example. Both plans have stairs, but another cabin might have only a ladder leading to the loft.

Figure 40 is a simple two-room plan. The larger room, with the fireplace, is for family living. The smaller room, for sleeping, would be cold in winter, but would receive some warmth from the larger room.

Figure 41, with three rooms, is called the Quaker plan or the Penn plan because William Penn, the famous Quaker founder of Philadelphia, recommended it to his colonists. Quakers who came to North Carolina brought the plan with them.

Figure 42 shows a center hall plan, a great advance toward privacy and better living. The hall, as may be seen, permits entry and movement in the house from one room to another without using any room for passage. This is the plan of the brick Newbold-White house, previously discussed (figure 33), and so is shown with thick walls. This design is called a "primitive" example of the center hall plan, for two reasons: the hall is quite narrow, strictly a passage, and not overly pleasant; and the stairway, although entered from the hall,

FIGURE 42.

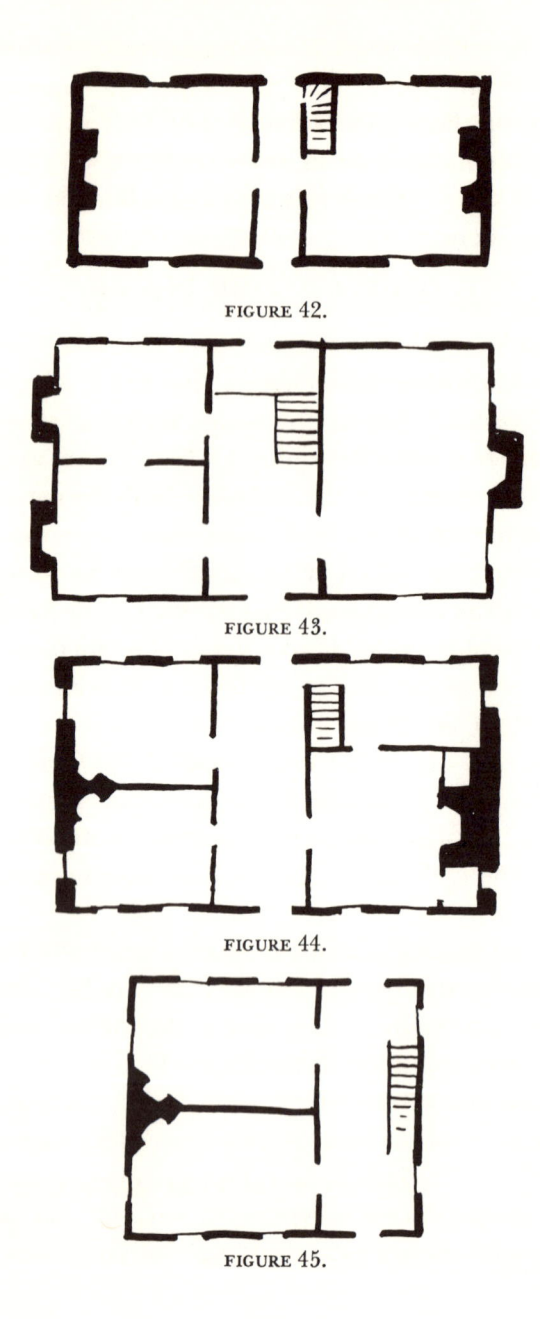

FIGURE 43.

FIGURE 44.

FIGURE 45.

remains within space which belongs to an adjoining room.

Figure 43 shows a developed center hall, a wide and pleasant place in which to linger. The stairway, now within the hall, is not boxed in—as in the example above, but stands in open space. It rises half a flight to a landing which runs across the hall; the upper half of the stairway, of course, is not shown in this first floor plan. Looking at the three downstairs rooms, one recognizes the Quaker plan in grand, developed form, with a fireplace in each room.

Figure 44 shows a four-room plan and also serves to suggest the small variations and special features which may be incorporated into any plan. The drawing represents the original plan of the Old Brick House, already noted, (figure 35), and is based upon information from the present owners. Reading from left to right, there are back-to-back corner fireplaces on the left wall, both served by one chimney, thus economizing on masonry costs. The central hall is wide, but no open stairway is mounted there; instead, the boxed-in stair is located in space stolen from a side room, as in plan 42, above. The main room at right has a fascinating chimney wall; a storage space on one side of the chimney is balanced on the other side by a closet with window. The famous carving which adorned this wall will be shown later.

Thinking of the exterior appearance of this house, and remembering that 18th-century men admired symmetry, note how each entrance door is centered on its façade, even though the hall is pushed slightly to one side. And note the quiet symmetry of the two windows on the right, serenely independent, yet obviously a determining factor in the combination of installations along the interior of this wall. Further, the flue to the off-center fireplace on this wall manages to work toward the center of the wall as it rises, so

FIGURE 46.

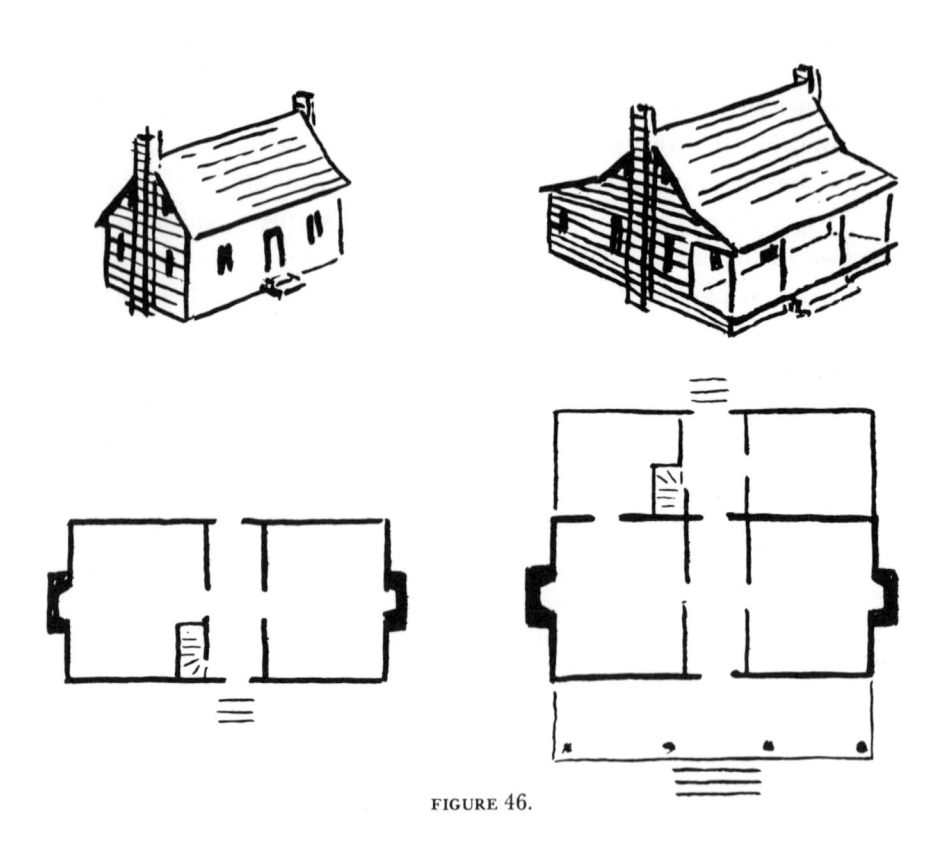

that it can emerge in a chimney properly centered to balance the chimney on the other side of the house.

Figure 45 shows a side hall plan. It is like a center hall house deprived of one of its wings. This design was popular in fine late 18th-century city houses, where the hall was an important show-place in the house. In our diagram the stair rises in a straight run.

The sketches above presented simple one-, two-, and three-room plans; then center hall plans with two, three, and four rooms. All these divisions of space were found within the basic rectangle enclosed by the outside walls of the house. Further divisions were used, too. For example, consider where the Palmer house (figure 14) fits into the plans seen in this discussion.

HOUSES WITH LEAN-TO AND BIG PORCH— —THE SOUTHERN HOUSE

Figure 46 shows a simple rectangular house on the left; on the right the structure has sprouted a lean-to in the rear and a porch across the front. These two sketches illustrate a common development in the expansion of the simple rectangular house. A lean-to simply "leans against" the main frame of the house. The porch, often a precarious structure on its delicate posts, depends for its support upon the stable frame of the main block of the house also.

While some owners of simple rectangular houses enlarged them by adding the lean-to and the big porch, other colonists, seeing the attractiveness of this plan, built the whole house, lean-to and porch, at one time.

In driving through North Carolina one sees hundreds of houses similar to the one on the right. It has been called the typical North Carolina farm house. It became popular in towns as well as on farms. The big porch sweeping across the front provided very welcome living space during the hot summer months, and the porch offered a sheltered place for children to play in during inclement weather.

It may be surmised that the colonists also appreciated a beauty in the design of this house. Where the earlier house on the left is boxy and stiff, the house on the right has a roof line that reaches out pleasantly from the center ridge to the front and back. The front porch looks inviting and friendly, like a room opening to the outside world. The other house, with only a stoop at the front door, is really closed to the world.

Consider the two houses as geometrical forms:— the first house is merely a simple block. By contrast, the expanded house has a more complicated geometrical nature for us to think about and enjoy. It can be described as a central block which has two, paired appendages, one of which is transparent.

Although the lean-to was found everywhere in the colonies, the big porch is of Southern origin. It was employed first in the North Carolina seacoast towns that conducted trade with the West Indies, where similar colonnaded porches existed.

Turning now to the plans shown in figure 46, it may be seen how the lean-to neatly adds two small rooms to the rear of the structure. The main hall of the house continues through the lean-to, and front and back doors give through-ventilation to this long "room." It was often the favorite place for family living during hot summer months. The stair in our plan begins in the back. However, there were many variations in the location of the stair and, indeed, in the use of this general design.

In figure 47 are shown some of the variations of the lean-to and porch design in North Carolina houses of greatly differing aspect. In figure 47a, the basic house has a gambrel roof. This

PLAN IDEAS—THE STUDY OF FLOOR PLANS 63

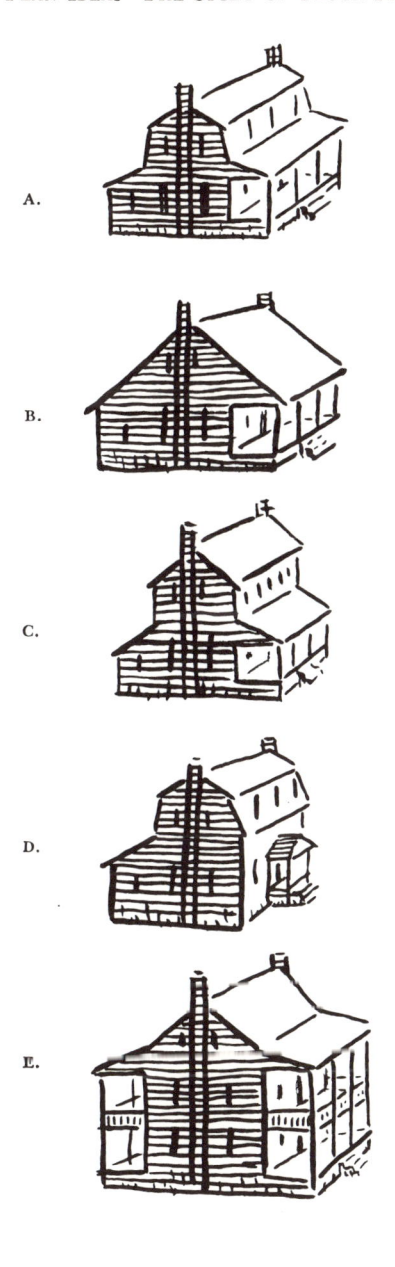

A.

B.

C.

D.

E.

FIGURE 47.

is particularly charming, with three crisp roof planes on either side of the central chimney. Beginning at front or back the roof planes fold up to the center ridge and then fold down again.

Figure *b* shows the whole house under one massive gable. It looks particularly strong in contrast to the movement and delicate grace of the roof in sketch *a*.

In sketch *c* the center block of the house pops up for two full stories, towering above the low porch and shed.

Sketch *d* shows a gambrel house with a lean-to but without a big porch sweeping across its front. This sketch is introduced to show that either the lean-to or the big front porch alone may occur on a house.

Sketch *e* shows two-tiered porches on both front and back. If one big porch is considered desirable, two—or four—are better. Two-tiered porches often are found on the great mansions and plantation houses. Such porches were also a feature of inns, providing ample sheltered space for guests and their friends. It is just one step from the two-tiered colonial porch shown here to the great porches of the early republican period (for example, Mount Vernon, of the 1780's) where giant columns or piers rose through two stories.

Having seen the sketches above, we now discuss a few actual houses which incorporate the lean-to and big porch design.

Figure 48, the Hummock house, exhibits one of the porches inspired by the West Indies which are characteristic of its town, the old port of Beaufort. The group of visitors in our photograph reflects the fame of this house which attracts sightseers to the town.

The house is called by several names: *Hummock, Hommock,* or *Hammock*. These unfamiliar words are variants

PLAN IDEAS—THE STUDY OF FLOOR PLANS 65

FIGURE 48. THE HUMMOCK HOUSE, BEAUFORT.

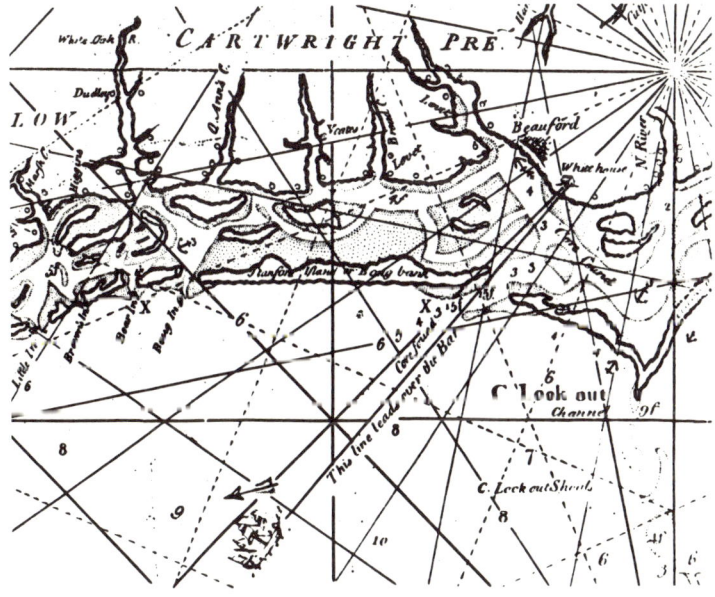

FIGURE 49. DETAIL FROM A MAP OF NORTH CAROLINA, 1738.

of, or are related to, the common word, *hillock;* and the house does stand on relatively high ground in the eastern part of present-day Beaufort. Years ago the house was called the White House, as old inhabitants remember. Today it is white for sure, its chimneys having been plastered over, it stands there gleaming, its two great dormer eyes staring out to the sea as if searching the horizon. And once, no doubt, pilots of ships at sea looked toward the land, seeking this white house to guide them through the narrow Beaufort channel.

Figure 49, a detail from James Wimble's mariners' map of "The Province of North Carolina," published in London in 1738, shows a ship lining itself up with the "White house." As recommended by Wimble whose purpose was to show mariners how to avoid sand bars and shallow water in finding their way to ports such as "Beauford," the line of sight from a ship at the point shown to the easily identifiable landmark leads over the bar. If this White house shown on the map is, indeed, the White House of present-day Beaufort, then it was built before 1738, the date of the map.

Figure 50 depicts a fragment of the foundation of the house. At left the great wooden sill rests upon a brick pier. A heavy cross beam is inserted into the sill and is held in place by two large wooden pegs with nicely carved heads. Out on the cross beam a joist is inserted, a sliver of wood being driven under the joist to bring it to proper height and snugness. This sketch evokes the vision of colonists with huge logs and simple hand tools engaged in the heroic project of building a house.

Figure 51 is a diagram of the foundations of the house; dotted lines encircle the fragment which was sketched above. Heavy lines show the major floor beams; a few lighter, parallel lines indicate joists. The heavy beams divide space

Plan Ideas—The Study of Floor Plans   67

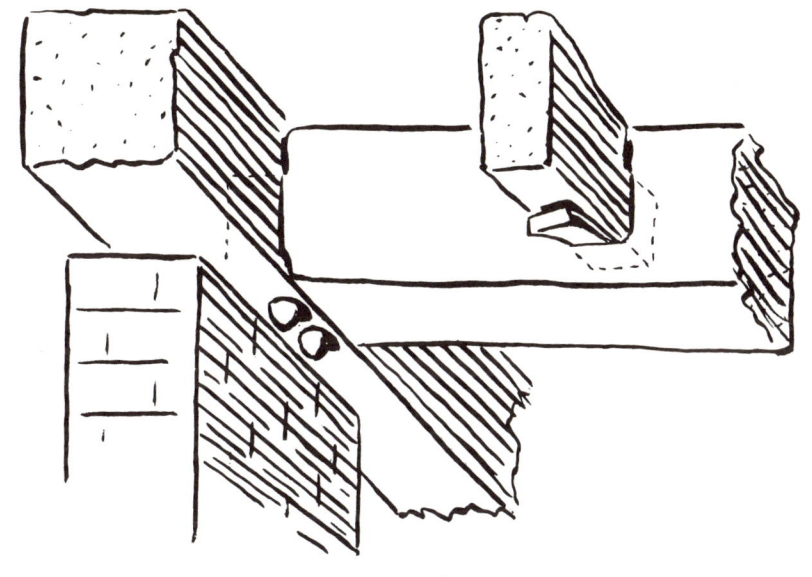

FIGURE 50.

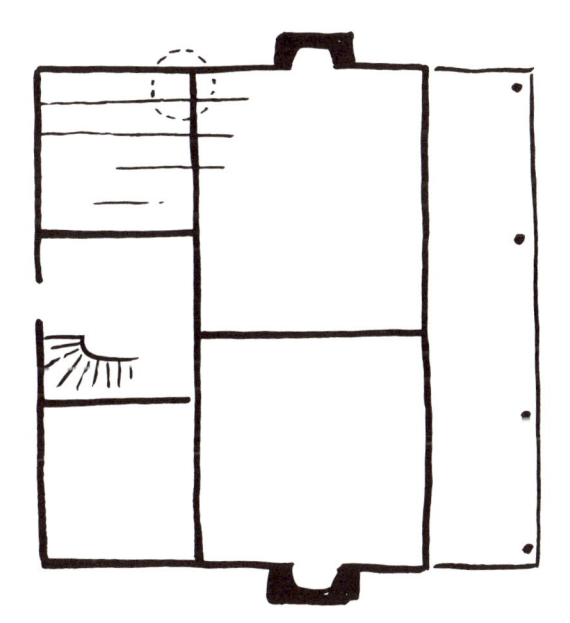

FIGURE 51.

in a way to suggest the lean-to design:—there are two front rooms, each with a fireplace at the middle of its wall, while the rear section contains a small room on either side of a hall in the center. In the diagram a stairway is included in the hall also. This is said to be the original stairway, since removed. Not shown in the diagram is the back porch, which appears to be a later addition.

The Sloop Point house (figure 52) is another well known house with a large porch. As much as any colonial house, it is filled with novelties and mysteries. Also known as the MacMillan house for the family which has owned it for well over one hundred years, the structure stands facing the Inland Waterway, at Sloop Point, just east of Wilmington. Construction is thought to date from the late 1720's.

Our photograph shows the impressive profile of the house, all under one great gable roof, the porch end resting on massive square piers. The chimney serves fireplaces in two adjoining rooms and recalls the double chimney previously seen in the Palmer house (figure 13). In the Palmer house closets were constructed between the twin fireplaces, but in the MacMillan house there are outside doors to first floor and to basement. The present porch between the fireplaces is a recent addition. The chimney is laid in Flemish bond and, as can be seen, the upper part of the chimney, blown off by a storm a few years ago, has been replaced with brick laid in our 20th-century fashion.

In figure 53 the single chimney on the other side of the house is shown. Below, the ballast stone base reveals a fascinating collection of beach stones and coral in many colors; above, the brick is laid in English bond which, as mentioned earlier, contains alternating courses of headers and stretchers. The different bonding systems used in the

Plan Ideas—The Study of Floor Plans 69

Figure 52. The Sloop Point House.

FIGURE 53. SLOOP POINT HOUSE CHIMNEY.

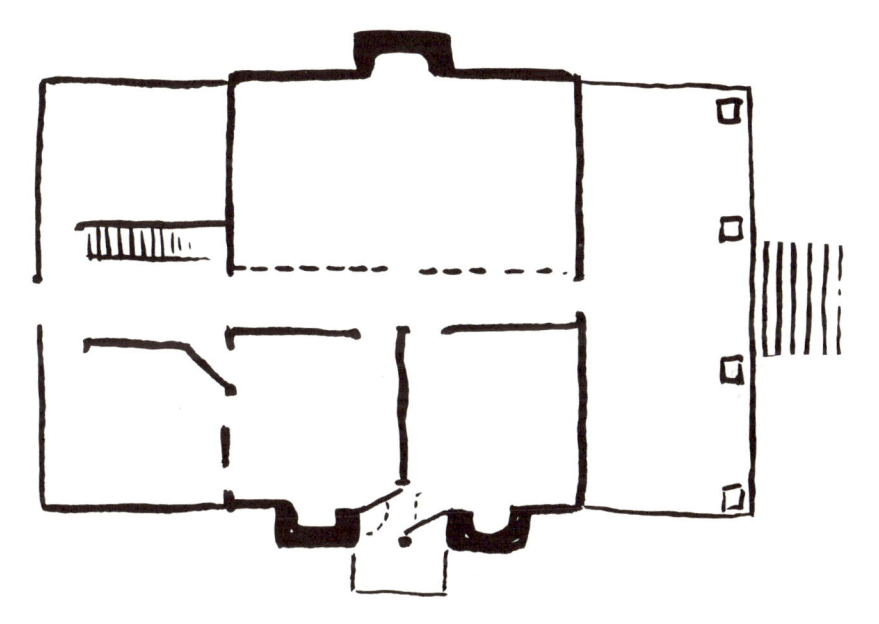

FIGURE 54. PLAN OF THE SLOOP POINT HOUSE.

two chimneys suggest that the chimneys were not built at the same time, which is one of the mysteries of the house.

Figure 54, a plan of the Sloop Point house, illustrates some of the novelties in the house. The designs of a central block, plus a big porch in front and a shed addition in the rear is readily apparent. The dotted line through the main block represents a partition which was installed during the 19th century to create a central hall. Before this addition, three rooms existed in simple Quaker plan. The hall is intended solely for service, being only about 3½ feet wide. When the partition wall was added no attempt was made to reproduce the original cornice and wainscot panelling of the big room.

Between the twin fireplaces unusual twin doors may be noted. They swing in and out from the corners of the fireplaces in such a fashion that one room at a time is opened to the porch. When both doors are swung out, there is passage between the two rooms. The twin room toward the back of the house has three doors along its rear wall; one leads to the hall; the other two are believed to have led to closets in the past.

Now we present two diagrams to aid in discussion of the growth of the Sloop Point house from an early, smaller structure (figure 55) to the house of today (figure 56). The roof of the house was raised or "lifted" in the early 19th century, according to one historian, but exactly what changes were introduced at that time is not now known. The "before and after" sketches are shown in order to demonstrate the extent to which the house has evolved since its original construction. Almost every old house shows evidence of changes; efforts to determine the reasons for these modifications can tell the student much about the fashions of times past and the character of the people who dwelled in the structure.

The smaller, earlier house is built over a low basement (suggested by dotted lines) the masonry walls of which serve as the foundation of the building. The light porch has delicate carved columns and a railing with banister posts. At its outer side the porch rests on masonry piers; at the inner side the porch's floor beams are inserted into the foundation wall of the house. Stucco, applied over the ballast stone foundations, has incised lines in imitation of stone blocks, as suggested in the diagram. Today fragments of this incised stucco may be seen here and there on the front and side foundations.

The larger, present-day house with raised roof (figure 56) has full-height second story rooms in the main block of the house and additional space in front and back. Details *P* and *R* indicate parts of the construction which use lumber

PLAN IDEAS—THE STUDY OF FLOOR PLANS 73

FIGURE 55.

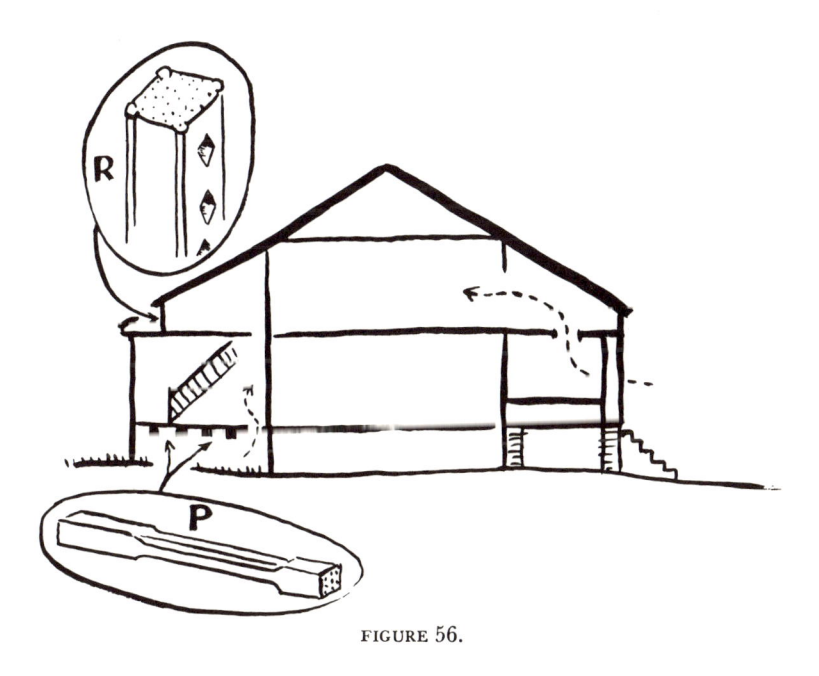

FIGURE 56.

salvaged from some previous structure. *P* shows where four carved porch posts are used as floor beams. *R* indicates three banister rails used as studs in the back wall of an upper room. Both the posts and the banister rails could have come from an earlier porch on this house. The present porch uses massive posts to support the heavy roof. To support the porch on its house side, brick piers have been added in front of the original ballast stone foundations. There are other details of the house which suggest stages in its development; we hope someone will study them someday.

To return to further examination of the curiosities suggested in diagram 56, dotted lines are shown to represent the flow of air through an ingenious cooling system. Toward the back of the house a hole in the floor allows air to rise from underneath to ventilate a bedroom. At the front of the house, an opening in the porch ceiling allows air to rise to a closet on the second floor front, and thence to bedrooms.

One last unusual detail is the stairway in the back hall, the banister posts of which are set diagonally, that is, perpendicular to the hand rail rather than the steps.

Figure 57, a drawing of a house from Brunswick Town, near Wilmington, introduces an amazing new chapter in the story of colonial architecture in North Carolina, a chapter which is just being opened up in our day.

This house, the Hepburn-Reonalds house, built between 1734 and 1742, is of a type not seen before in this study. The structure had a family porch without steps down to the street, rather like a balcony, a protected place to sit and look at life on the street. Below, in the basement was a shop, and in the illustration a man is seen about to enter the street door of the shop.

Unfortunately, the house does not exist today; the drawing is "conjectural," that is, it is an estimate based upon study

FIGURE 57. CONJECTURAL DRAWING OF THE HEPBURN-REONALDS HOUSE, BRUNSWICK TOWN.

FIGURE 58. RUIN OF THE HEPBURN-REONALDS HOUSE.

76   COLONIAL HOMES IN NORTH CAROLINA

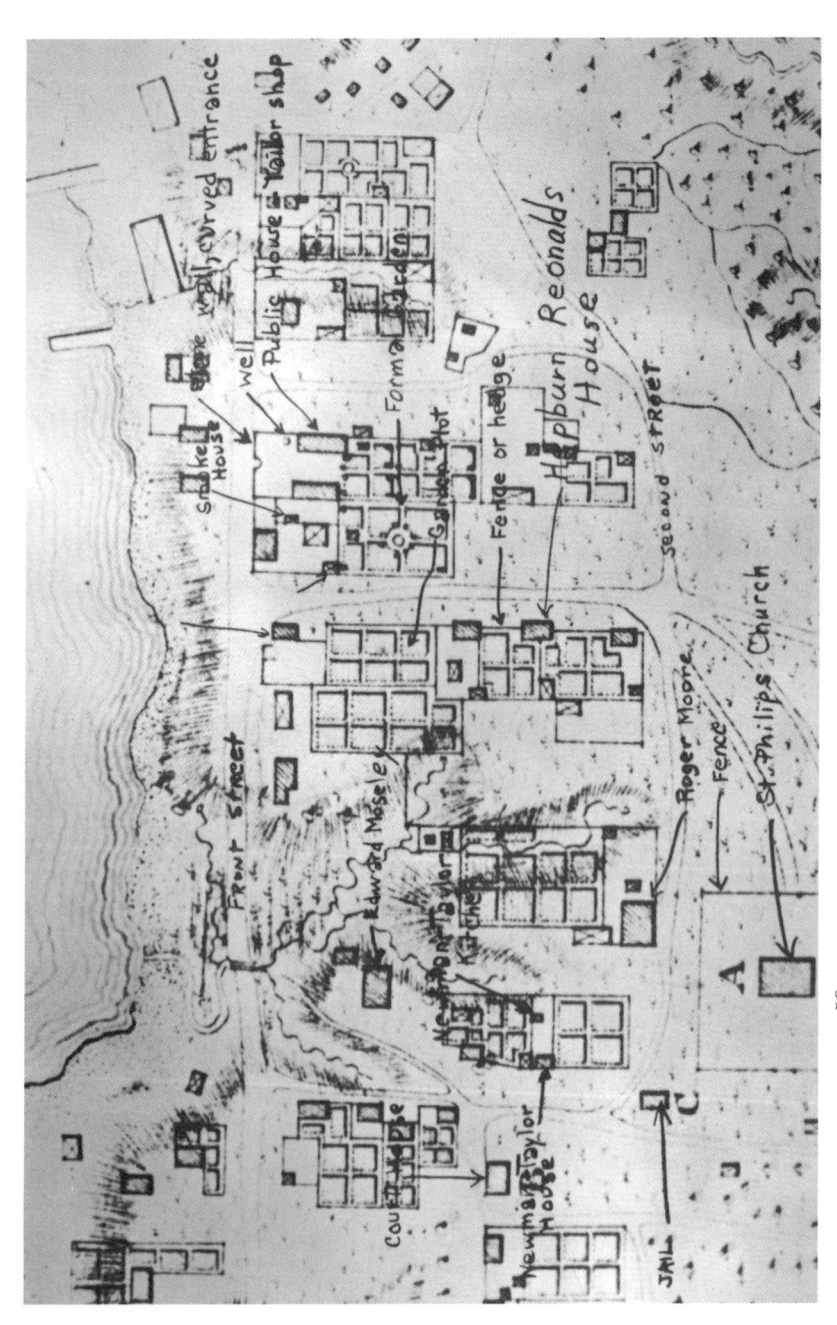

FIGURE 59. DETAIL FROM SAUTHIER'S DRAWING OF BRUNSWICK TOWN IN 1769.

and analysis of ruins (figure 58) at Brunswick Town. Knowledge of this kind of house in North Carolina, and of the town is a dramatic development of the last few years.

Brunswick Town, founded in 1726, was a thriving port town in colonial times, as might be imagined from the map (figure 59), a detail from Sauthier's drawing of Brunswick Town in 1769. At the time of the Revolution the town was burned and fell to ruins. During the War between the States, many bricks and stones were taken from Brunswick Town's ruins for use in the construction of Fort Anderson, adjacent to the town site. Our photograph of the ruins of the Hepburn-Reonalds house shows this—one may see that many of the stones and bricks from the chimneys have been removed. During the century after the war the remaining foundations of the town's buildings all but disappeared into the ground, being covered by washes of soil and dense jungle of brush and trees. Only the great brick walls of St. Philip's Church (marked "A" in the map) remained as a reminder of the once thriving town. In 1958, however, the State Department of Archives and History began a project to clear the land, dig out the foundations of houses, and search for objects left by the colonists, all in order to recover an image of the town and the way of life of its citizens.

Thus far some sixty ruins have been discovered by the archaeologist in charge of the work. In digging around a ruin he works very carefully; all the soil removed is sifted, thereby bringing to light coins, buckles, broken pottery, door hinges, and other items. Some of the richest finds have been uncovered in garbage and refuse pits.

While the work of the archaeologist continues, Brunswick Town has been opened to the public as an open air museum—quite an unusual exhibit, one found in few places in the world. As one walks down the streets there are display cases at individual ruins. The cases contain objects found at the site, as well as drawings of houses as they probably looked before burning.

One of the most interesting of Brunswick Town's houses is the Hepburn-Reonalds house. According to Stanley South, archaeologist in charge,

> the second floor porch was an architectural feature borrowed from the West Indies, where this style of architecture was popular. Many of the homes in Brunswick were of this type, with a cellar partly sunk below the surface of the ground and a garret above the main floor of the house.

If the photograph and drawing are examined carefully, the steps which lead down and the path to the basement door may be seen. The photograph also reveals the remaining foundations for the posts which supported the porch. The basement is divided into two rooms; the nearer room was a kitchen which was entered from the rear of the house.

On the Sauthier map (figure 59) the Hepburn-Reonalds house is marked by an arrow. Looking carefully at the map one sees indications of certain details shown in the drawing, such as the fence running along the street, the barn and garden, and the fence leading to the barn. The drawing was made by Don Mayhew, staff artist of the Brunswick Town project.

One question the reader may have in mind: how does one know the name and date of this house? Very complete records of the sale of property in Brunswick Town have been preserved in nearby Wilmington and Southport. By careful study of these records and of the Sauthier map it has been possible for the archaeologist to identify and date the various ruins in the town.

Wakefield (figure 60) is the oldest house in Raleigh. It was built in 1760 by Joel Lane, who later sold the original tract

FIGURE 60. WAKEFIELD, RALEIGH.

of 1,000 acres of land for the new state capital. The sale, it is said, took place in this house on Joel Lane's farm. The house was moved a few years ago to its present site—not far from its original location—and now is owned and maintained by the Wake County Colonial Dames.

As the photograph shows, it is a gambrel house with shed addition in the rear, but, unlike houses we have just been discussing, it has only a small porch in front. It is probable that the house originally looked quite differently, for construction details in the vicinity of the roof suggest that it once had a gable roof. Further, the smooth sheathing over the front of the house (often found under the porches of colonial homes) suggests that originally a shed porch ran across the entire front of the house. With long porch and gable roof, Wakefield would have looked like the typical farm shown in the sketch, figure 46.

In the Joel Lane house as it stands today, the porch, the chimneys, and the modern shingles differ slightly in design from those elements seen in old photographs and drawings of the dwelling. In the back of the house, barely noticeable in the photograph, is an addition beyond the lean-to. This later appendage was once attached to the left side of the house; in its present relocation it is occupied by the caretaker of this exhibition house.

Figure 61 shows plans, elevations and details of Wakefield. Such careful drawings are the sort which present-day architects prepare for the use of carpenters building a house. While the colonial architect or builder did not make such elaborate drawings, the plans of important old buildings, are today being made as an historical record. The drawings shown are from a collection being developed at State College, Raleigh, further explained at the end of this booklet.

The first floor plan at lower right shows the porch, the

PLAN IDEAS—THE STUDY OF FLOOR PLANS 81

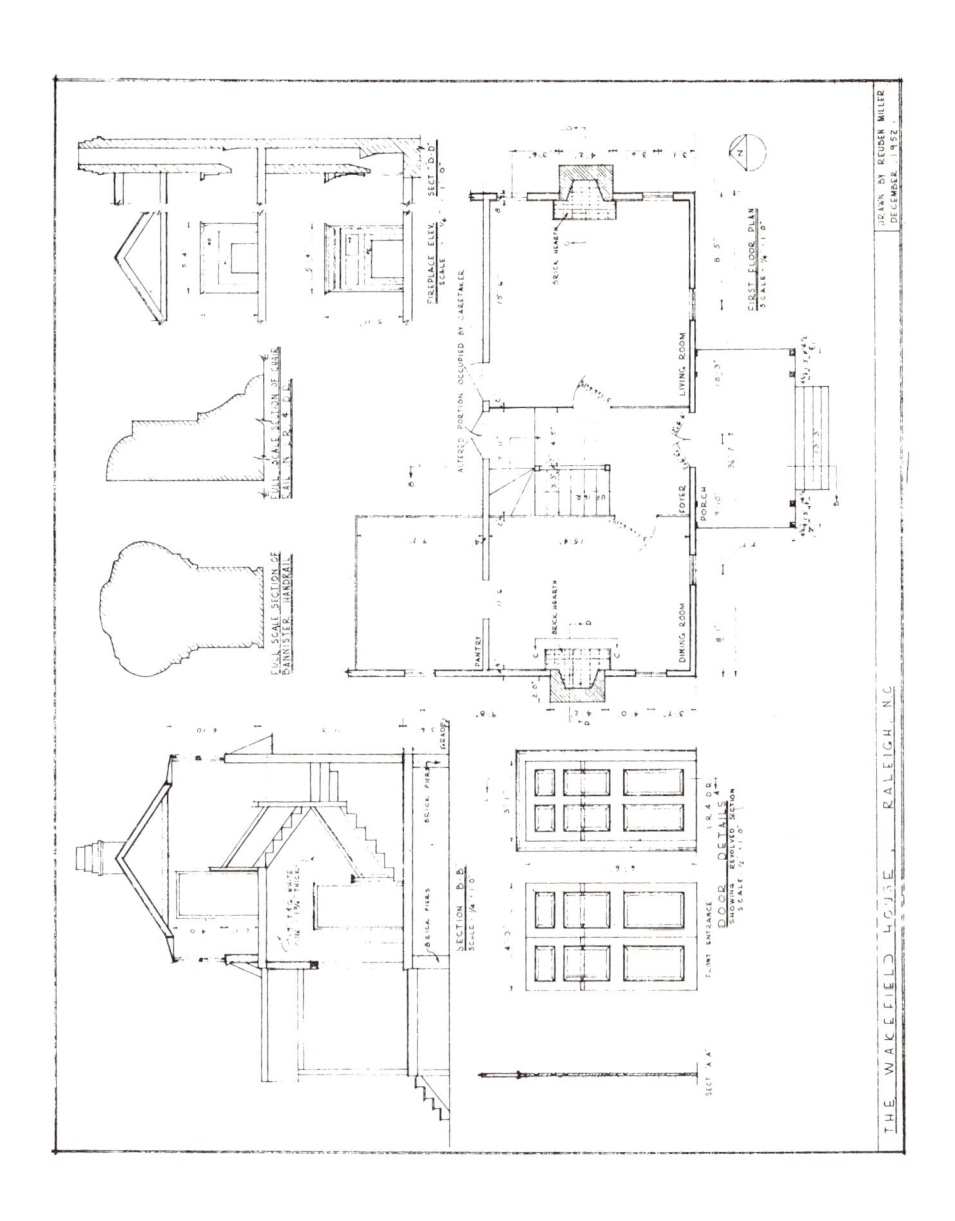

FIGURE 61. WAKEFIELD, MEASURED DRAWINGS FROM THE PROJECT IN HISTORIC ARCHITECTURE RESEARCH, STATE COLLEGE, RALEIGH.

main block of the house, and a room of the lean-to in rear. In the main block are a larger and a smaller side room, with a hall between. The entrances at front and back of the hall are wide double doors, facilitating good ventilation during hot summer days in Raleigh. The door to the larger room is centered "as it should be"; but the corresponding door to the opposite room has necessarily been pushed forward by the stairway. It will be noted that whereas the outer framed walls of the house are fairly thick, the walls which partition the hall are extremely thin—a point which will be discussed presently.

At upper left in the page of drawings is a transverse section through the hall. We see how the stairway folds neatly within the main block of the house as it rises. The stair has a railing, but no procession of banister posts, thus bespeaking an economy and rugged plainness—but a visitor must watch his step. At the top, the stair ends in an upper hall lighted by a dormer window. At the back is a corresponding dormer. As our drawing is a section through these windows, it does not give an immediately clear notion of the gambrel roof. However, just beneath each window can be seen part of the lower plane of the roof.

Figure 62 shows the large front room of Wakefield, as restored and furnished by the Colonial Dames. The room with one wall of plaster and the other of wood, looks almost "modern." The wood wall showed in the plan as very thin, as we have noted. The similar wood partition on the other side of the hall shows through the open door. To have covered these partition walls with plaster would have been quite an additional expense to the builder; and so one finds that the "modern" effect is in reality a by-product of simple economy. Looking carefully at the open door on the left, one notes the small wooden pegs which lock the horizontal and vertical frame members together.

FIGURE 62. INTERIOR OF WAKEFIELD.

CHAPTER V

Interiors

The interior from Wakefield, just seen (figure 62), represents one idea about how the walls of a room should be treated. There were other schemes for the treatment of the main room of a house; some of these are illustrated in figure 63 and in the following sketches.

In figure 63 parts of the great frame of a wooden house project unashamedly through the smooth plaster walls and ceiling. Running across the middle of the ceiling is the large center beam of the house. A similar member along the outside edge of the ceiling might be expected to continue all the way around the room as a cornice, but it does not. At the floor line, however, a base board does continue around the room, but it is heavier under the window wall. The chair rail (the board or rail installed about the height of the back of chair, to protect the plaster from damage) does continue around the room, but at the corner it develops special bracing not employed where the rail joins the frame of the door.

Such irregular features suggest a skeleton of the house going beyond the present room. The builder of this dwelling was unconcerned if one wall was different from another—

FIGURE 63.

FIGURE 64.

perhaps he felt a keen satisfaction in the wooden structure of his house and was pleased to have this framework reflected in the interior. This spirit is occasionally seen in the less important rooms of a colonial house (for example in the Palmer house), but it is rarely found in the main rooms of extant colonial homes.

Figure 64, also a simple interior, is more expressive of what colonial builders desired. The cornice, the chair rail, and the base board continue around corners without any change in character. Thus the room appears as a box having its own order, independent of irregularities in the frame of the house. Chair rail and base board are almost always found, because they were necessary to protect the plaster. The cornice, although occasionally missing, is usually present—as though the builders felt it was necessary to mark the upper edge of the cube of the room. The fireplace is adorned with surrounding panels. A fireplace is psychologically an important place in the room—it is the source of warmth and the place where people gather—and, therefore, it is honored with special decoration.

A more elaborate interior is shown in figure 65. The mantelpiece rises to the ceiling and has some carved details. A paneled wood wainscot runs around the lower part of the wall. The inset sketch shows a long plank sometimes used in the wainscot, and left exposed as a long panel. The front is glassy smooth, the back is rough hewn and notched to fit snugly against the upright posts. Such a long panel of wood is not overly impressive when used today—it is just a sheet of plywood—but in a colonial house it is something to awe a modern carpenter.

Figure 66 shows an exceptionally elaborate room inspired, perhaps, by pattern books or memories of England. The mantelpiece is an elaborate concoction of many units piled

FIGURE 65.

FIGURE 66.

one on top of the other—ledges, columns, a gable pediment—a display of the carver's skill. The walls are fully covered by a series of vertical panels above and horizontal panels below.

Having seen in the above sketches some of the notions which colonial builders had for finishing the important rooms in a house, we will look at photographs of two fully paneled rooms, one plain and the other elaborately carved.

Figure 67 is an interior from the Lane house, Nixonton, shown as an example of a simple, fully paneled room. This Nixonton house is the second Lane house to be discussed in this study; the first was Wakefield, the Joel Lane dwelling in Raleigh. Our photograph shows one of three rooms from the Nixonton Lane house, as now installed in the Carolina Room at the University of North Carolina. This is the section of the University library which contains books, pamphlets, old photographs and newspapers, all referring to North Carolina. It seems appropriate that the Lane interiors should be at this center for studies of North Carolina history and culture. The installation was accomplished under the direction of Thomas Waterman, student and author of works on North Carolina architecture.

The over-all design of the room shown consists of panels set in a lattice of vertical and horizontal strips. Window height determines the three-part division of the wall—tall vertical panels in the middle, and short horizontal panels above and below. This scheme is repeated in smaller scale at the mantel. The emotionally important fireplace is given a few further touches of embellishment—a carved mantel shelf and pilasters at the edges above. (A *pilaster* is a rectangular support treated as a column with a base, shaft, and capital.)

Figure 68 is inserted into our account at this point to aid in discussion of a special beauty in this room, the expression of a craftsman-builder. The drawing shows a section of the

INTERIORS 89

FIGURE 68. INTERIOR OF THE LANE HOUSE, NIXONTON, AS INSTALLED IN THE CAROLINA ROOM, IN THE LIBRARY OF THE UNIVERSITY OF NORTH CAROLINA.

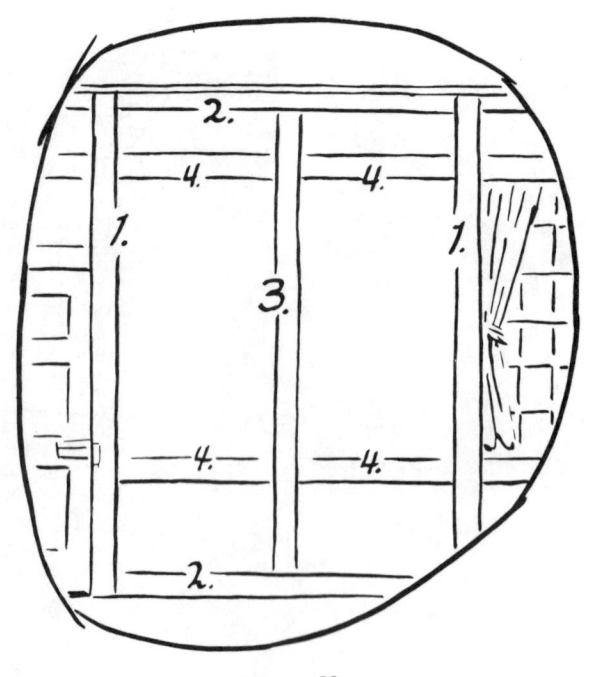

FIGURE 68.

wall in the photograph. In his actual construction of the paneling, it appears that the craftsman followed these steps: *1st)* erected uprights marked 1 and 1, which rise all the way from floor to ceiling, corresponding to the posts which frame door and window; *2nd)* cut and fit the strips marked 2 and 2, which fit neatly between the uprights; *3rd)* erected the secondary upright marked 3; *4th)* fitted in the short pieces marked 4, the location of these strips being determined by the framing of the window. The above sequence of steps is the natural, rule-of-thumb way to proceed; the craftsman does not need a blue print—or even a ruler. Thus the wall expresses the craftsman-builder at work, suggests his simple procedures and his delight with his material, wood, whose satiny surface is brought out in the room.

INTERIORS

FIGURE 69. THE LANE HOUSE NIXONTON.

Figure 69 shows a sketch and a plan of the Lane house at Nixonton. It is a simple one-story building which looks down peacefully on the Little River. Sometimes it is called the Old Customs House, or the Old River House. It is dated in the 1740's, some years before the other Lane house, Wakefield, in Raleigh.

The plan of the house is a clean-cut example of the three room idea advocated by William Penn. The big room was seen in our photograph (figure 67). The two smaller rooms had walls of plaster. Foundations above ground are of brick; below ground are the stone walls of a low cellar. It may be remarked that there is no stair to the loft. The loft window shown in the sketch was "just for looks," according to old settlers. Today, however, the loft is reached via an addition to the house, not shown in the sketch.

Figure 70, an interior from the earlier mentioned Old Brick House, is shown as an example of an elaborately paneled room. It was put into the Old Brick House about mid 18th century, at about the time of the simple Lane interior, just seen above. It is opulent, high-spirited, robust. Perhaps its swashbuckling grandeur would appeal to a pirate and could, therefore, be used to support the legend that Blackbeard once lived in this house. The legend, however, is unfounded; Blackbeard had been dead for many years before this room was executed, and similar interiors are found in other North Carolina houses known to have been built by highly respectable owners.

The Old Brick interior stands in sharp contrast to the chaste Lane interior. Whereas the Lane interior expresses simple wood structure, as we have seen, the Old Brick interior suggest stone. The row of energetic pilasters support a very convincing "stone" architrave above, and the arches are constructed complete with keystones as found in stone work.

INTERIORS 93

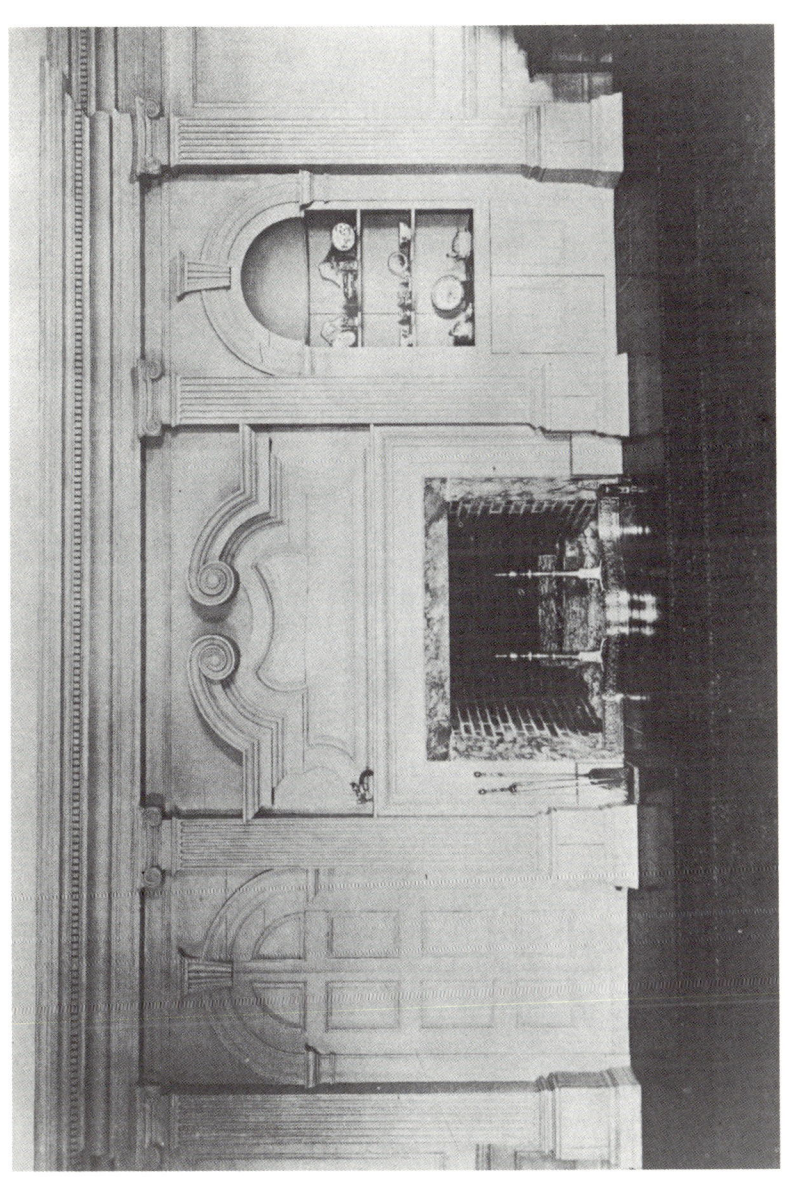

FIGURE 70. INTERIOR FOR THE OLD BRICK HOUSE.

94 COLONIAL HOMES IN NORTH CAROLINA

FIGURE 71. INTERIOR, THE OLD BRICK HOUSE IN ORIGINAL SETTING.

The Old Brick House's interior has left North Carolina. The photograph shown portrays the fireplace wall as it is installed in a house in Delaware, its proportions changed to make it fit a higher room. An older photograph, figure 71, shows the door along the wall in the original room. By comparing the before-and-after photographs it can be seen how blocks were inserted under the pilasters to accommodate them to the height of the room and providing more head room above the arch. In the original room the pilasters stood emphatically "on the ground." The door proudly "raised itself to its full height," the keystone of its arch touching the enframement above. The more the two photographs are compared, the greater the appreciation one has for the particular nature of the original room, and the intention of its designer. It had a dynamic pride, in contrast with a politeness which characterizes the later room.

The re-installed room has also changed the original arrangement of parts along the wall—the door, the mantelpiece, and the cabinet. The original arrangement of these units may be seen by looking carefully at figure 71, and also the plan of the Old Brick House, figure 44.

CHAPTER VI

A Note on Later Colonial Architecture

The scope of this booklet does not include architecture of the late colonial and early republican times, although some of our most distinguished "colonial" buildings date from those years. The architectural climate of the late 18th century differed from that found prior to 1763. First of all, following the end of the French and Indian War the colonies were more secure. Then, these existed a large body of earlier architecture which could be seen as accomplished fact. The building trades were more firmly established, a few professional architects were beginning to appear, and architectural pattern books and design books were more available from Europe. Although the earlier buildings were vigorous in their design, the wealthy person who wished to build a home in later colonial times often looked on them as quaint and a little clumsy; he wanted something better and more up-to-date.

An outstanding example of what was up-to-date in North Carolina, is shown above, an engraving of Tryon Palace, New Bern. This structure was begun by Governor Tryon in 1767, completed in 1770 and destroyed by fire shortly after the Revolutionary War. The work of reconstruction, begun in 1952 is now virtually complete, and the palace is now one of the most widely known colonial buildings in the United States. It is a good example for our present purposes because, as a most important and costly building, it reflects ideas regarded as "modern" in North Carolina at the close of the pre-revolutionary period. The engraving shown is from *The Pictorial Field Book of the Revolution,* by Benjamin J. Lossing, 1852. Although the palace was in ruins during Lossing's time, he made his engraving from drawings left by the building's architect—the same drawings used in 1952 for its reconstruction. The palace was designed to impress the colonial man and woman shown in the illustration in certain ways, as will be seen presently.

The exterior of the palace exhibits something new in our study: a three-part layout design, diagrammed in figure 72. Above in the diagram the three structures are arranged: kitchen—PALACE—stables. Other outbuildings which, of course, were present are hidden in the first and main view of the palace. This is quite different from the disposition of the outbuildings at the Palmer-Marsh house (figure 9), where they are found informally situated at one side of the house.

At the middle of the diagram depicting the Tryon structure, the long façade of the palace building is shown broken into three parts: wing—CENTRAL BLOCK—wing. The central block is crowned with a pediment and is advanced slightly forward. The Palmer house also has six windows and a central door, but the builder of this earlier structure did not have the idea of breaking or articulating a long wall as in the palace.

Below in the diagram, the central block of the palace

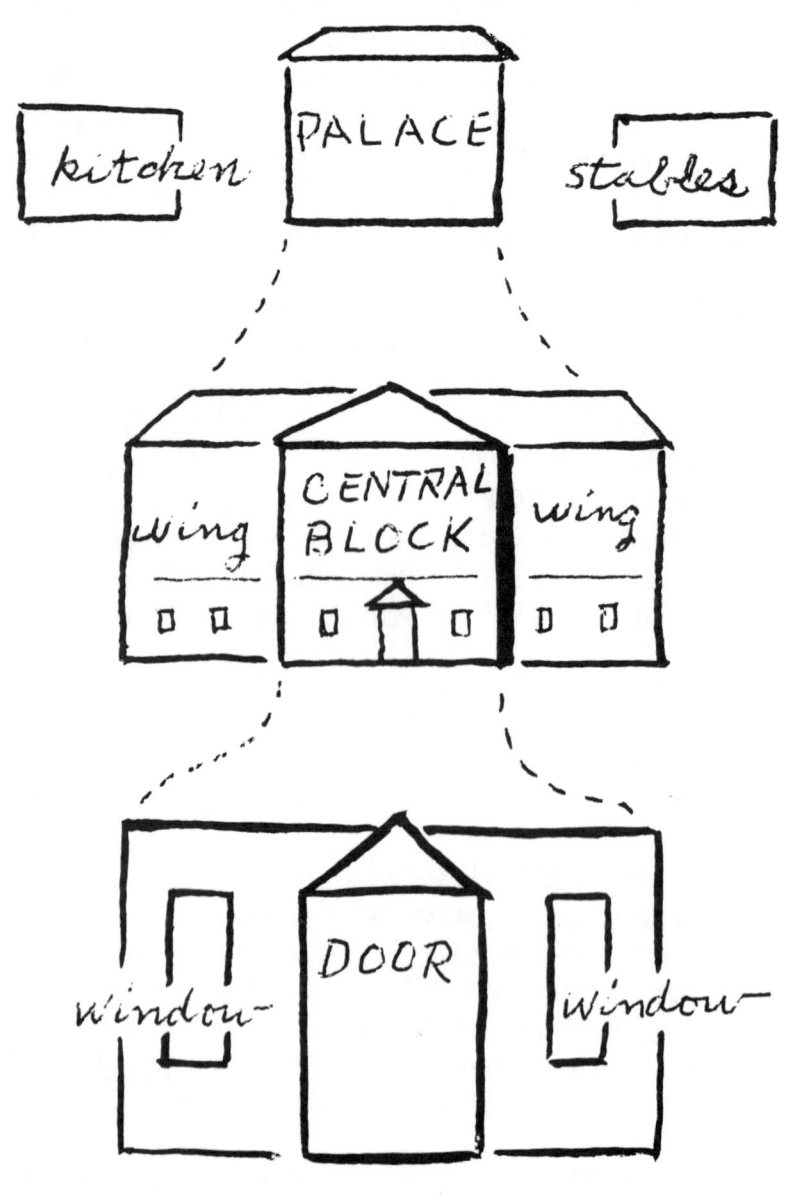

FIGURE 72.

shows window—DOOR—window. That door, crowned with pediment, is the ultimate focal point.

As one contemplates this three-part idea for dividing a length of wall, or for grouping separate structures, the system seems to express an "intelligence" in the architecture—the door or middle unit being a head or center of serene intelligence and the symmetrical side units being arms or body. This design idea was not introduced into the colonies via the palace; the palace merely demonstrates the idea which became so attractive to later 18th-century builders.

The two pediments referred to above—a big one above and a small one over the door below—are not mere gables of the sort seen earlier. Instead, they are complete, three-sided pediments similar to those found on classical temples. They are a sign of a rising interest in classical art, fostered by archaeological studies in the 18th century. Classical buildings also contained ideas of sober mass and order which impressed those who lived in the late 18th century.

It should be observed that the cornices of all three buildings continue uninterruptedly around corners, marking a firm top for the lower part of the buildings which appear as great boxes. Further, as all the buildings have hipped roofs which retreat on all sides, the colonial man and woman in the picture, as they come near a building, do not see a roof at all. This image is in contrast with the earlier architecture with huge, steep roofs sitting like massive hats on the buildings, and with gable ends rising to sharp points in the sky, along with their protruding chimneys. At the palace, chimneys do not disturb the calm surface of a rectangular wall, and roofs are hidden as though one is ashamed of them.

The windows of the palace are in absolutely regular horizontal and vertical rows, as opposed to the casual, hit-or-miss irregularities seen in some earlier buildings. In preparing his drawings for the façade of the palace, the architect must have erased and redrawn his windows before he achieved just the rhythm and balance he wanted. In looking at his drawing he saw the façade as an entity by itself, exactly as it was seen by the colonial couple on the walk. They seem to feel the articulate order of the building, a security and a restrained, aristocratic elegance.

Such ideas afford one a glimpse into the proud, ambitious, "enlightened," later 18th century. After this glimpse we return to the diverse buildings of the earlier 18th century, with fuller appreciation of their robustness and good-natured vitality, each building seeming something of heroic accomplishment, a feat of colonial man, which, indeed, it was.

CHAPTER VII

The Study of Old Architecture

Aside from pleasure to be derived from it, the study of old buildings can be of great value to future students of North Carolina architecture. An important old building in one's town today may be a filling station tomorrow. Every day such buildings vanish through fire or demolition and often there are no adequate records of them. Such records can only be made by people on the spot who appreciate their importance.

Steps that can be taken by the student include: making a study of an old building in the vicinity; taking photographs of various exterior views and interior details; making plan drawings with measurements; making simple sketches and diagrams of construction details which cannot be photographed well; and making a plot plan or map of the property, showing the location of former sheds and other structures. In addition, efforts should be made to collect information from old inhabitants and from present users of the building. Deeds, old letters, or other documents should be consulted for information regarding the structure's origins. A map of the old part of your town—*à la Sauthier*—might be a useful contribution to supplement information on the founding of the town and on changes as they have occurred.

Such studies would be valuable additions to a collection of documents, photographs, maps etc., housed in the local library. Work with teachers, librarians, and members of the local historical society to build a collection of books and material on local and regional architecture.

There are several State institutions in Raleigh which may provide assistance with projects of this kind. The Department of Archives and History, houses a vast collection of documents and letters, and publishes the *North Carolina*

Historical Review. Within this department the Hall of History sponsors the *Junior Historians,* who make models of buildings and engage in other architectural projects; and the Historic Sites Division is concerned with the preservation of important sites and buildings. The Department of Conservation and Development has a photograph collection of old buildings in North Carolina. The School of Design at State College has a growing collection of measured drawings of important old buildings; this project is called Historic Buildings Research (see figure 61).

In Chapel Hill, at the University of North Carolina there are two sections of the library to be noted: the Carolina Room, which houses extensive collections of historical materials (see page 88) ; and the Southern Historical Collection, which contains letters and documents. Duke University has large collections of documentary material; and other college and city libraries have North Carolina collections.

A NOTE ON BIBLIOGRAPHY

A most useful book is *The North Carolina Guide,* edited by Blackwell P. Robinson, published by the University of North Carolina Press, 1955. Professor Louise Hall, Duke University, wrote the excellent architectural section of this book.

Two attractive and important books are illustrated with photographs by a woman master photographer to accompany texts prepared by a man:—*Old Homes and Gardens of North Carolina,* photographs by Bayard Wootten, historical text by Archibald Henderson, published under the auspices of The Garden Club of North Carolina by the University of North Carolina Press, 1939; and *The Early Architecture of North Carolina, a Pictorial Survey,* by Frances Benjamin Johnston with *An Architectural History,* by Thomas Waterman, University of North Carolina Press, 1941. *The State* is a magazine published in Raleigh; it has special issues devoted to towns and regions of North Carolina, containing much standard and new information.

Three general reference books should be noted: *The Dwellings of Colonial America,* by Thomas Waterman, University of North Carolina Press, 1950 *The Architecture of the Old South,* by Henry Chandlee Forman, Harvard University Press, 1948. *Early American Architecture,* by Hugh Morrison, Oxford University Press, 1952.